AF488205

5 Simple Habits
for
Successful Change

Making Your Change Journey Fun, Fast, and Effective.

www.5HabitsForChange.com

Copyright 2025 by

Todd Musig and Gary Dansie

Published at Cottonwood Heights, Utah

ISBN 979-8-9940638-3-5

Library of Congress Control Number: 2024925273

Who is This Book For?

This book is for those who want to make positive changes in their personal and professional lives. Change is 24/7 for everyone.

These 5 Simple Habits empower you to achieve better results from every change you make.

If you are an organizational leader, you now have new tools to keep the team raving about change while you keep the work environment up-to-date and productive.

This Book Uses the Adult Learning Approach

K-12 schools use a pedagogical approach to learning, where the teacher directs the learning. Children are passive, like sponges, ready to absorb new information on every topic.

That approach doesn't work for adults. Adults already know many topics, especially those related to job skills, so that the pedagogical approach could be monotonous and useless.

This book is structured using the "Adult Learning" approach.

You will be familiar with the concepts. But as you read, you can apply what you know to solve problems, generate ideas, and discuss these concepts with others.

How can that all happen from a flat piece of paper? We've added exercises and quizzes for you to solve.

We encourage you to take a break in your reading and complete the exercises. Personalize the exercises with experiences from your life to make the concepts meaningful.

---Gail Sheehy---
If we don't change,
we don't grow.
If we don't grow,
we aren't really living.

Contents

You hear about

Artificial Intelligence (AI)

Crypto

Stable Coin

&

Smart Contracts

but

None of these can solve your

Change Project for you.

The

5 Simple Habits for Successful Change

Mindset

Will help you change easily!

Introduction

What most organizations or people struggle with isn't change strategy—it's execution, buy-in, and momentum. Initiatives stall. Teams resist. Leaders push harder. Individuals flounder in personal life.

Imagine a change where people understand the destination and want to be part of the success in their job or in their personal life.

The 5 Simple Habits for Successful Change give your organization or yourself a simple, repeatable way to move change forward—faster, with less friction, and better results.

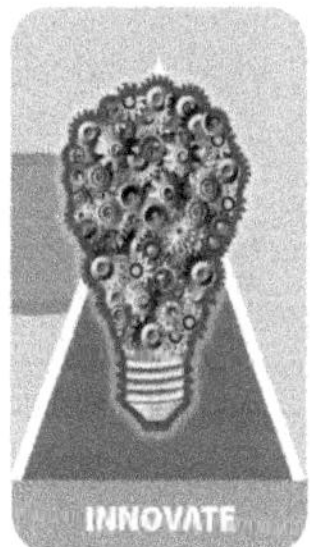

This isn't a program that adds more work. It's a mindset that helps you or your people do the work they're already doing—more clearly and effectively.

We Want to Share With You

We wrote this book because we've lived through Change—sometimes as leaders, sometimes as team members, as consultants, and also as individuals.

Between us, we've spent decades working inside organizations, consulting leaders, coaching teams, and writing about what makes people more effective.

We hope this book inspires your best in the future.

Chapter 1

HABIT 1 - **ITERATE** the Change Journey

Change is a Journey

Change isn't instant. You don't jump from start to finish. Change is a journey that takes time and will be full of pitfalls and successes. The results could range from impressive to a total disaster.

Practice As You Learn

Can you think of a change that backfired, was abandoned, or rolled back to the old way of doing things? Identify three reasons it failed.

What Does the Word "Iterate" Have to do With Change?

A Change Journey consists of several separate activities or tasks. We'll call these separate activities **"Iterations."**

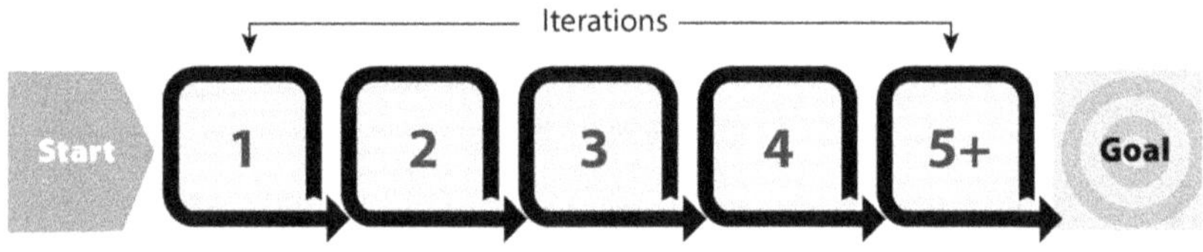

You will soon see that **"Iterate"** (verb) and **"Iterations"** (Noun) are the best words to describe a successful Change Journey. **Iterations** are dynamic, flexible, and fun. The process will learn from itself, like AI, and get better as it moves forward.

Word Semantics

The word(s) you use to describe something is/are critical if you want to convey a clear understanding to others.

When you discuss "**Iterate** and **Iterations**" with your team, it's a new approach for them that will lead to some fun "outside the box" thinking. Getting the team involved ensures success.

It's like sprinkling magic dust on the journey to accelerate success.

Change requires flexibility, so avoid using words like these:

Steps: If you call them "**Steps,**" you describe a structured activity that is NOT flexible. Going up and down stairs requires consistent step construction, or you may trip or fall! Local building codes require consistency when constructing steps.

Pieces: How about the word **"Pieces?"** If you hit a rock with a hammer, the pieces are chaotic and scattered—not a good attribute for your change.

Tasks: Using the word **"Tasks"** for the journey oversimplifies the effort needed.

Each Iteration is a Dynamic Self-Contained Process

An **Iteration** can be portrayed as shown below.

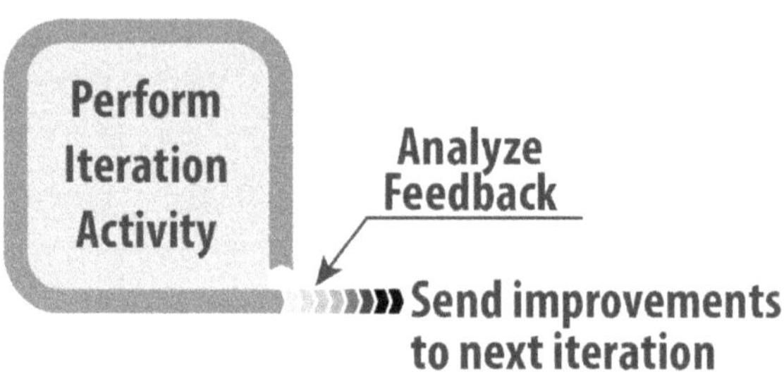

1) ACTIVITY: Your team performs the activity described by the **Project Plan**, plus any adjustments recommended by the previous **Iteration**.

2) ANALYZE FEEDBACK: When complete, you analyze feedback and determine how the next **Iteration** can be improved.

3) ADJUST THE NEXT ITERATION: Then send a message to the next **Iteration** on how to do the activity better.

4) CELEBRATE: And finally, have a little **Celebration** for what you accomplished and learned---even if it's a pat on the back.

IMPORTANT

*You can **Plan** the **Iteration** in advance, but you must be willing to adjust the next **Iteration** based on what you learn from feedback.*

Iterations are Sequential

Look at the **Iteration** in the Change Journey. When one **Iteration** is complete, you perform the next **Iteration** sequentially.

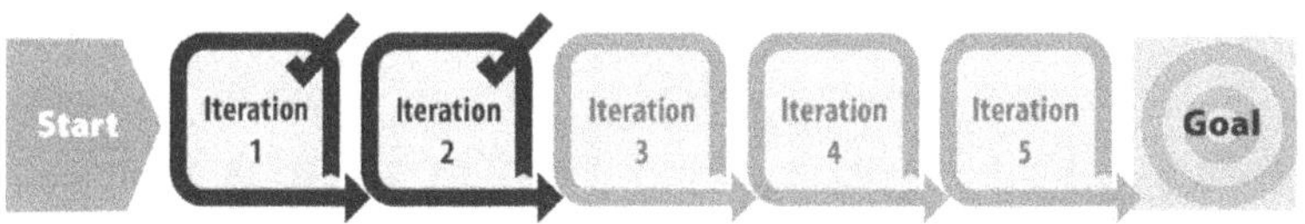

Each **Iteration** learns from the previous and shares advice with the next in line. The Change Journey teaches itself to accomplish more, faster.

How Many Iterations Does a Project Need?

Each project should have more than one **Iteration**. If there is only one, you lose the advantage of feedback and course correction along the journey. Anytime an **Iteration** becomes large, take smaller bites.

> *It's the old question, "How do you eat an elephant?"*
> *The answer--*
> *"One bite at a time."*

Change Journey vs. Iterations

Can you drive from Denver to Cincinnati nonstop for 17 hours in one **Iteration**? Of course not! You'll stop for gas or battery charging, restroom breaks, food, etc. Looking back, how many **Iterations** was the journey broken into?

And remember how good it feels when, many hours later, you see the sign "Welcome to Cincinnati." What do you do then---You **Celebrate**!

Large Change Projects May Need to be Broken into Phases

It may be beneficial to break large projects into sub-projects or phases, each with its own Goal, **Project Plan**, and **Iterations.** A change may require several distinct phases, such as (1) Research, (2) Procurement/ Logistics, (3) Implementation, and finally (4) training. Each phase contains **Iterations**.

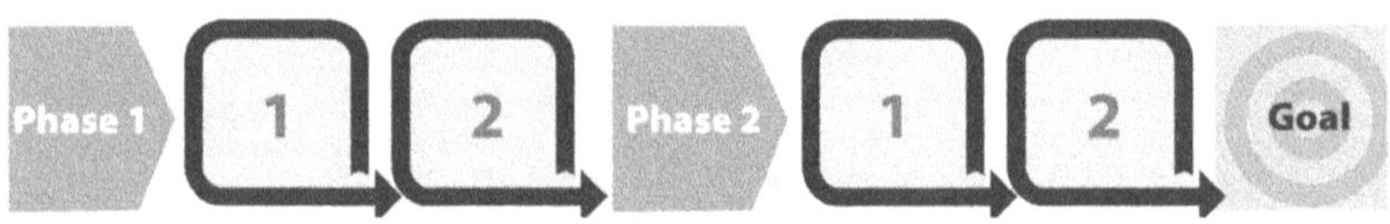

Parallel Projects

The Master **Plan** may call for several sub-projects to run in parallel.

An example may be when several locations are implementing and training simultaneously. If you do, let one location lead slightly to give feedback to the others.

Don't get too far ahead, or you'll lose the advantage of cross-feedback between locations.

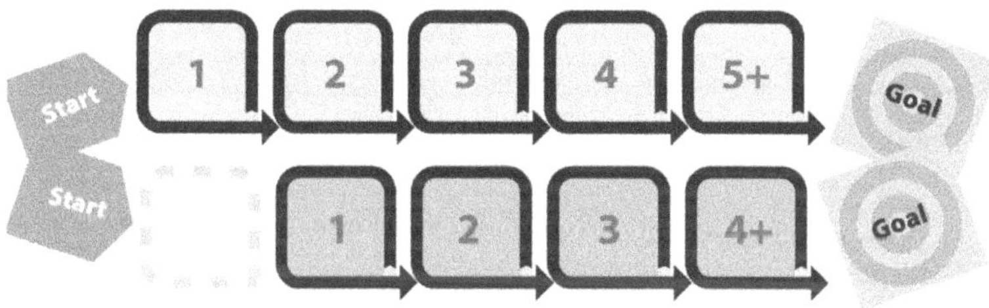

	Year	Principal	Rate	Return	Iterate	Piggy Bank
	1	$ 1,000	4%	$ 40	$ 1,040	$ 1,000
	2	$ 2,040	9%	$ 184	$ 2,224	$ 2,000
	3	$ 3,224	9%	$ 290	$ 3,514	$ 3,000
	4	$ 4,514	9%	$ 406	$ 4,920	$ 4,000
	5	$ 5,920	3%	$ 178	$ 6,098	$ 5,000
	6	$ 7,098	4%	$ 284	$ 7,381	$ 6,000
	7	$ 8,381	8%	$ 671	$ 9,052	$ 7,000
Met $10,000 Goal >	8	$ 10,052	8%	$ 804	$ 10,856	$ 8,000
	9	$ 11,856	6%	$ 711	$ 12,568	$ 9,000
Exceeded Goal >	10	$ 13,568	8%	$1,085	$ 14,653	$ 10,000

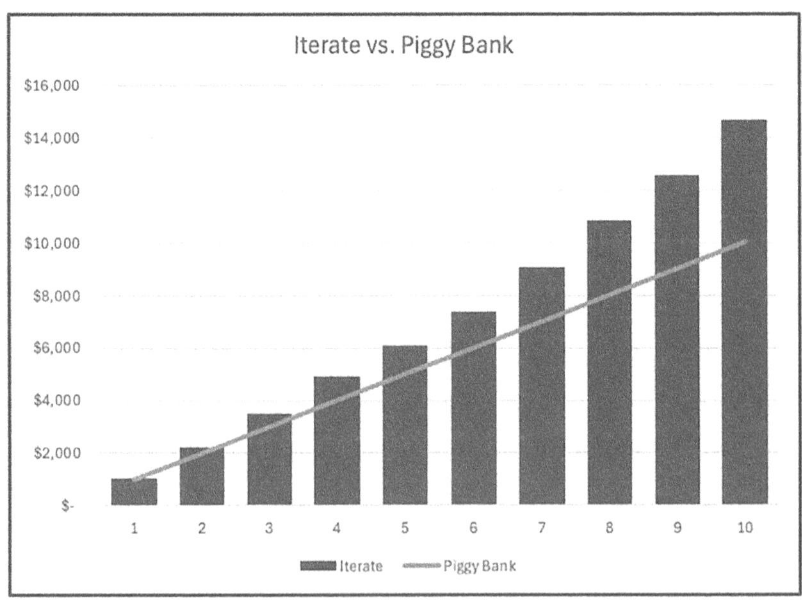

Iteration is Like Compounding Interest

Suppose your goal is to save $10,000 over the next ten years. It's simple: You put $1,000 in your piggy bank each year, and at the end of 10 years, you have $10,000. You have met your goal exactly.

Using the **Iteration Habit,** you put the first $1,000 into a savings account that earns you 4% interest. At the end of the first year (**Iteration**), you have $1,040 instead of $1,000.

Next, you analyze the results and find an investment that will earn more. You see a structured note paying 9% and so you put the $1,040 plus the 2nd year $1,000 ($2,040 total) into this new investment. At the end of the second year, you now have $2,224 compared to $2,000 using the piggy bank method.

The chart shows the power of **Iterating** each year, compounding your return even after adjusting for the economy's ups and downs affecting the annual returns.

The **Iteration Habit** resulted in two significant milestones:

    1- You reached your $10,000 goal in year 8 instead of 10 years.

    2- After 10 years, you have exceeded your goal by $4,653.

Using the **Iteration** Habit, your change project can compound it's success also!

Learning Iteration from a Slinky

Have you ever played with a slinky spring toy? Richard James invented it in the early 1940s.

Each loop of the spring seems to possess an internal inertia that pulls it forward until the last loop leapfrogs across, starting another set of gyrations.

Consider each loop one **Iteration** moving forward and adjusting smoothly until all the **Iterations** are complete. Can you imagine an **Innovative Project Plan** running smoothly like a slinky?

The 5 Habit mindset will make your change project run as smoothly as a slinky.

> *You might want to buy a Slinky (or a bunch of Slinkys) to demonstrate the 5 Habits Mindset to your team!*

Multi-level Iterations

A football game is an example of multi-layer **Iteration** at work:

Level 1 Iterations – First Half < > Second Half

At the end of the first half, the teams head to the locker rooms to analyze and readjust their **Plans** for the second half. Their analysis is intense because a lot is at stake to win the game—money, prestige, endorsements, etc.

Level 2 Iterations – Ball Possession Changes

Each time the ball possession changes, the offensive and defensive players swap places on the field. The players go to the bench for another analysis and instruction on adjusting their play the next time they are on the field.

If you watch closely, the defensive and offensive coaches carry iPads and may show the players on the bench video replays of what went wrong or right.

Level 3 Iterations – After Each Play

But the best coaches know they must analyze and adjust after each play. It's quick, with only seconds between.

Which Level is most important?

All of the levels are important. Each has a specific function in the Game towards success.

Iterate - Iterate - Iterate

Flexible Iterations

Sometimes, the number of **Iterations** remains flexible. The success of one **Iteration** determines whether another is even needed. Here's a story about an amateur baker who didn't know whether another **Iteration** was needed until he opened the oven door.

> ➜ *During my first try at making baguettes, the crust was too hard. So, I tried again (**Iteration** #2 putting a pan of water in the oven to create humidity and soften the crust. The crust was better, but after watching YouTube videos about shaping the dough and several more **Iterations** (#3, 4, 5), my Baguettes looked and tasted OK. I was proud to bake and deliver a batch to the neighbors.*
>
> *Then I went to France, where I ate an authentic baguette and felt like a failure! So, I tried to study what made the French baguette better. They made it seem so easy.*
>
> *Back home, I still couldn't match the French baguettes. One recipe recommended using French flour because their wheat has a different consistency than wheat grown elsewhere.!*
>
> *But I don't feel too bad because my baguettes are as good as those I've eaten in other countries, so I still bake them.*
>
> *However, I'm looking forward to another trip to France soon!* ←

Feedback to Improve the Next Iteration

When you complete an **Iteration**, analyze whether you met the expectations. Did it stay on course? If not, make **Innovative** adjustments to improve the next **Iteration**.

This simple story will illustrate how to use feedback and **Innovation** to improve the next day (**Iteration**).

> ➜ *A contractor (Dan) hired a crew to frame a new house. On the first day, Dan watched the crew run back and forth to their saws sitting next to the project's temporary power outlet.*
>
> *Dan asked the supervisor if they had longer extension cords. The supervisor admitted they had no more cords, so Dan bought more extension cords.*
>
> *The next day, with longer extension cords, the crew moved their saws closer to where they worked and framed twice as much as the first day.* ←

Here's what Dan did. He analyzed the output of day one, discovered a limiting factor, and then fixed it by buying more extension cords. He **Innovated** a simple solution. Sure, Dan spent $50 on new cords, but more extension cords allowed the crew to be twice as productive.

Since Dan pays the crew by the hour, the ROI (Return on Investment) was well worth the effort and expense.

Key Takeaways from this Chapter

- The Change Journey is sliced into **Iterations**
- Each **Iteration** teaches the next **Iteration** how to do it better
- **Celebrate** each **Iteration**!

Final Practice As You Learn

Open Google and search for the term **"Iterate."** Read an article that appears in the search. Think about how you can apply the **Iteration** technique in a Change Journey that you are working on at work or home!

Self-Assessment

Rate yourself on a scale of 1-5 (1=low, 5=high)

*1- I think through the **Iterations** needed to complete a small project.*

1------2------3------4------5

*2- I create a written simple **Project Plan** with **Iterations** for my change projects.*

1------2------3------4------5

*3- I seek input from my team before designing the **Iterations** for a **Project Plan**.*

1------2------3------4------5

The Iteration Habit will Empower Change to Succeed.

Chapter 2

HABIT 2 - **VISION** Success

Here is the word semantics again! You hear the word "Goal" daily. The goal is to change this or change that. For example, the company's goal this week is to ship 500 products. Goals usually describe metrics such as quotas or physical completion. However, stating a number goal is not glamorous.

Instead, convert the word Goal into a word with more appeal—**Vision**! A **Vision** is much more than just metrics. It includes benefits, intangibles, and deadlines, teases the senses, and gives you a reason to **Celebrate**!

The **Vision** is your destination. It's a goal on steroids. It's a colorful picture of what you want to accomplish. It should be emotionally charged and so appealing that everyone wants to help make the change!

The wording you use in a **Vision** can make a big difference. For example, instead of describing a **Vision** in metrics (e.g., the number of people trained), describe it with emotion: "the number of lives changed"—and you have a more powerful **Vision**.

Your new **Vision** defines the exciting and effective Change Journey you will be embarking on.

Converting a Goal into a Vision

Compare these goals to the corresponding **Vision**. Which version makes you want to be part of the experience?

Goal	Vision
Go to a posh restaurant in New York.	Enjoy the incredible ambiance at the Jean-Georges restaurant while experiencing the impeccable, mouth-watering five-course cuisine with a glass of $300 wine before the end of the month.
Go to a professional football game.	Experience the thrill of sitting on the front row of a professional football game, watching the teams battling to score early in the season with mustard dripping from the hot dog you're eating.
Install new software.	By the end of the month, experience the increased productivity of the easy-to-use new electronic document software. Eliminate the problem of finding paper records, messy desks, and everyone griping about who has the latest version.

As you can see, a **Vision** describes a total experience. It expands an otherwise dull goal into many beautiful possibilities and includes the deadline.

Remember this advice when creating a **Vision**. "Always sell Benefits, not the Features," is taught by top marketing and sales gurus like David Ogilvy, Seth Godin, and Ann Handley. This phrase emphasizes the importance of focusing on what the customer or employee gets from it rather than its cleverness or technical specifications.

Practice As You Learn

Let's pause while you practice turning these goals into dynamic **Visions** that excite and motivate your team or family. Don't forget to be creative and **Innovative** as you think about this exercise.

Goal	Vision
Eat a potato	(Describe Your **Vision!**)
Make extra money	(Describe Your **Vision!**)
Take a day off	(Describe Your **Vision!**)

How many times did you **Iterate** on each of your answers to make them better?

A Vision is Not the Project Plan

A **Vision** is not a **Project Plan**! It does not describe features or details about the process, describe **Iterations**, or assign tasks. It does include some metrics, like the deadline, but they are minor parts of the total **Vision**.

"Five Whys" Helps You Turn A Goal Into a Vision

"Five Whys" is a tool for figuring out the root cause of a problem or the real reason behind a goal. Knowing the root (problem or purpose) is essential when converting a goal into a **Vision**, or the **Vision** will send you to the wrong results. This technique was developed by Sakichi Toyoda, the founder of Toyoda Industries, in the 1930s.

The process is to ask "why" and then question the answer with another "why" four more times. Here's how it was used at the Jefferson Memorial in Washington, DC. The goal was to stop deterioration, but the real **Vision** is to keep the memorial beautiful for millions of visitors to enjoy in the future.

	Ask Why	Answer
1	Why is the Jefferson Memorial deteriorating, creating expensive repairs?	Because it is power-washed every two weeks.
2	Why is it power-washed so often?	Because of bird droppings.
3	Why are there so many bird droppings?	Because the birds come to feed on the small insects.
4	Why are there so many insects?	Because the insects come out at night.
5	Why do they come out at night?	Because the insects are attracted to the lights.

Once the nighttime lights were determined to be the root cause, the timers were reset so that the lights turned off before midnight. With the lights out, the bugs and birds went somewhere else, thus reducing the original problem of excessive bird droppings that required bi-weekly power washing.

The Value of Researching with Tools Like the Five Whys

Change Journeys usually require money and human resources and temporarily disrupt workflow. The best way to validate that you have the correct goal is to do some research. The more you understand the real purpose and benefits behind the goal, the better your **Vision** and Change Journey will become. The research will validate that you have the correct destination in sight.

> *Have you ever been given GPS directions and ended up in the wrong place? Did you double check the destination before you headed out?*

The Five Whys technique is one of many tools for gathering research about the **Vision**.

Practice as You Leaarn

If you were the head of the National Parks facilities department and were told to keep the Jefferson Memorial beautiful for millions of visitors, which approach would allow for a more **Innovative** solution?

Goal: Clean the bird dropping off the Jefferson Memorial ASAP.

Solution: Send a crew to power wash the memorial today.

or

Vision: Find a way to keep the Jefferson Memorial sparkling clean for three million visitors a year to enjoy while spending the least amount of the department budget.

Solution: Use "Five Whys," research alternatives, and design an **Innovative Project Plan** to accomplish the **Vision**.

You won't always be solving a problem but instead improving a process. The Five Whys is an excellent tool for determining the real purpose behind the **Vision**. A better understanding of the purpose results in a more effective **Vision** to guide the Change Journey.

Why is Creating a Clear Vision so Important?

1. People need to know where the change is headed.

2. People need to acknowledge that the change is necessary.

3. People need to be willing to support and participate in the change.

4. People waste time working on the symptoms, creating unnecessary tasks, or fixing the wrong problem.

5. People need more confidence in their ability to change.

6. People jump to solutions that have worked in the past and miss out on **Innovative** new opportunities.

7. People can be lazy and don't want to rock the boat.

8. Leaders often think they can convince people to support them by simply saying, "We are doing this because I said so."

Example of an Exciting Vision at Work

➜ *After his executive meeting, the Vice President of Marketing set a goal of developing five ideas to generate new sales leads. In a team meeting, he asked his busy employees to come up with ideas for next week's meeting. The following week came, and only a few token ideas were presented.*

The results would have changed if the leader had a better understanding of the power of a clear **Vision***.*

One idea would be to create a **Vision** *board that shows what more sales could mean to each person. Incentives could include trips, golf clubs, and even cash!*

At next week's marketing meeting, he could introduce the **Vision** *board and ask each person to share what they would do with an extra $5,000 bonus next quarter. Of course, everyone would be excited to participate. To put the icing on the cake, he might offer $500 for the three top ideas voted on by the team.*

The next meeting would be flooded with practical, actionable ideas because, as a team, they now shared the **Vision** *of what more sales leads could mean personally.* ⬅

When you share an exciting **Vision** with your team, family, or friends, the momentum builds quickly because the **Vision** comes with personal rewards.

Example of an Exciting Vision at Home

➜ *Chuck and Mira are saving for an anniversary trip to Costa Rica in two years. They created a **Vision** and posted a picture of a Costa Rican beach on their bathroom mirror. They look at their **Vision** at least every morning and evening. The picture pumps them up about the trip!*

*The trip will cost about $5,000. So, Chuck and Mira broke the $5,000 into twenty-four monthly periods (**Iterations.**) Chuck is in a bonus pool at work that pays out every 30 days. They decided that Chuck's bonus money would go into savings for the trip.*

*After nine months (nine **Iterations**), the savings were $200 short of the **Plan**. To stay on track, they decided to skip buying tickets to a concert and use the ticket money to catch up on their savings.* ⬅

The "Vision Habit" will ensure that they achieve their Vision of lounging in the warm Costa Rican sun on a fabulous beach.

Recruit Your Team's Help Turning a Goal into an Exciting Vision

Expanding a goal into a full **Vision** is fun, especially when you involve your team and let each person generate their own personal "buy-in" to the **Vision**! Make the **Visioning** effort memorable for everyone, including yourself.

Creating a good **Vision** will require several **Iterations**.

Useful Mnemonic - S.P.A.C.E.

Here's a mnemonic for using the word "space" that might give you more ideas on how to create a clear **Vision**.

S	Specific	Be specific about benefits and timeline.
P	Present	Portray the desired state in the present.
A	Action	Make sure the **Vision** is actionable.
C	Color	Think of a color movie instead of a movie in black and white.
E	Emotion	Help all workers and stakeholders become excited about the potential coming soon.

Be sure to let the project team contribute upfront. Their participation will improve buy-in as they understand the purpose behind the **Vision** and what's in it for them. Nobody wants to put extra effort into something they haven't had input into or don't understand. Remember, "Sell the benefits, not the features."

The next time you are assigned a project, turn the goal into a **Vision** and share it with the people working on it. Also, please share it with all stakeholders for feedback. Nothing is worse than solving a problem different from what the stakeholders expect—then it's back to square one.

Make a Vision Board or Bulletin Board

Have you ever created a **Vision** board or bulletin board where you post pictures of your **Vision**? Some people like to tear pictures from magazines or print them online.

Your personal **Vision** board might feature a picture of Hawaii because you are saving money to go there for your anniversary. Mirrors and refrigerator doors are good places to post images, so you will see your future fun daily!

A **Vision** board or Scoreboard in the office benefits work projects by ensuring the entire team buys into the **Vision**.

If you can't show a picture, perhaps post the benefits or a graphic showing the completion percentage and update it weekly. Be sure to include a picture of the **Celebration** your team will have when the project is completed.

> **A VISION expands a Goal into an exciting future state that people love being involved in.**

Key Takeaways from this Chapter

- A **Vision** is an exciting picture of the future.

- A beautiful **Vision** motivates your team.

- A clear **Vision** makes project **Planning** easier and more effective.

- A successful **Vision** represents the collective thinking and feedback of a team and gets stakeholders in sync.

Final Practice As You Learn

Think of a change you want to make at work or in your life. Write a **Vision** statement (not a goal statement) and discuss it with a friend or your team for feedback. Don't forget to add a picture where you can.

Quick Quiz

How many of these attributes are included in a Vision?

[ ] Be Specific.
[ ] Express the desired state in the present tense.
[ ] Make sure the **Vision** is Actionable.
[ ] Make the **Vision** Colorful-include the senses.
[ ] Include Emotion to make it exciting.
[ ] Deadline.
[ ] Share the purpose with all stakeholders.
[ ] Encourage **Innovation** and feedback.

**All choices are essential when creating a good Vision. Take a moment and consider what might be missing when you are creating a Vision for yourself or your team.

Chapter 3

HABIT 3 - **INNOVATE** Everything

There are many strategies for how successful change occurs. Most of the time, change is painful for both the organization and those affected by the change. Everyone usually appreciates the benefits of the change after it has occurred, but change is often begrudged while in the middle of it.

Changes made with the 5 Habits for Change follow a new approach. Each **Iteration** gathers feedback, and then it's time to be creative and **Innovate** ways to improve the next **Iteration**. The **Innovation** Habit is a key to creating enthusiastic participation.

This chapter will demonstrate how **Innovation** empowers everyone to accomplish goals well beyond expectations.

Let's Talk About Creating and Innovating.

According to the dictionary...

Create means:	**Innovate means:**
"To bring (something) into existence."	"To change something established, especially by introducing new methods, ideas, or products."

This new mindset encourages you to create something new, **Innovate**, enhance, modify, exemplify, adjust, experiment, refine, or do all these things.

Is Creativity and Innovation Being Smothered?

Here is a fascinating study to consider.

> ➜ *A study in the 1960s commissioned by NASA found that 98% of five-year-olds scored at a "genius" level in creativity tests. By age 15, only 12% scored "genius," while adult study participants dropped to 2%. Educational theorists argue that traditional education methods have taught us to "color inside the lines" instead of thinking as creators and **Innovators**. ⬅*

Has the "Change Journey" become too much like "coloring inside the lines" and lost effectiveness?

Useful Cliches

When you hear **"Think Outside the Box,"** does that conjure up a scenario where the boundaries are gone, leaving you free to roam in areas you've never explored?

And doesn't **"Color Outside the Lines"** sound like a directive to do something new and different from the norm?

That's precisely what is expected in the **Innovation** Mindset—No boundaries, go explore, be different! You don't need to be in the study's 2% genius score to have fun and be successful!

Why Does Coke Taste Better at McDonald's?

Many people think that a Coke® at McDonald's® tastes better than a Coke you buy elsewhere. Has Coca-Cola® developed a special formula exclusively for McDonald's? According to Coca-Cola, the formula is precisely the same for every customer.

Since Coca-Cola didn't "create" a new formula, what has McDonald's done to **"Innovate"** an exclusive flavor worldwide?

- The syrup concentrate is delivered in stainless steel containers that keep the syrup fresher than plastic.

- With 41,800 stores worldwide, that means 41,800 different flavors of water! To overcome that variation, McDonald's filters and chills the water used to dilute the concentrate. So, a Coke in Moab, Utah, is consistent with one you buy at McDonald's in Casablanca, Morocco.

- Next, they calculate the syrup ratio based on the melting ice in the cup. Even after the ice has melted, the last slurp still delivers full flavor.

- Finally, McDonald's provides wide straws so that more of the **"Innovative** flavor" hits the taste buds!

This is the kind of subtle, creative, and **Innovative** thinking you'll soon use to get consistent and superior results for your next Change Journey.

Become an Innovator

Anyone can learn the **Innovator** mindset. Think of great **Innovators** throughout history.

1900's

Did you know that Henry Ford, the **Innovator** of mass production of cars, began his career working for Thomas Edison, the **Innovator** of many things we use today?

1970's

How about the **Innovative** rivalry between Steve Jobs (Apple) and Bill Gates (Microsoft.) They certainly changed our lives.

2021

Or **Innovators** Elon Musk, Jeff Bezos, and Richard Branson's race to commercialize space travel. Do you think you'll ever travel in space? Why did these billionaires risk their lives to travel in their spacecraft? Because they believe in their **Innovations**!

Today

If we study the habits and actions of **Innovators**, we can become the **Innovators** of our change.

> *Believe that your **Innovations** will succeed.*

--- Yogi Bierra ---

*If you don't know
where you are
going, you'll end up
someplace else!*

Comfort Zone

Expanding Your Comfort Zone

You are often asked to do something outside your skill comfort zone. Do you **Innovate** and **Iterate** ways to expand your comfort zone or hold back and stumble your way through the assignment?

Pizza Dough is a great analogy!

Have you watched a new cook spin the dough to size the pizza crust? The dough starts small and begins stretching as it spins. It wobbles when it reaches the cook's comfort zone, but if the cook keeps spinning, it finally stretches to fit the pan.

After spinning a couple of dozen more crusts, the new cook finds the process easier, and the number of pizzas produced per hour increases.

A new cook starts with a small personal-sized pizza and, when it's mastered, moves on to the mid-size and finally the large size.

So, be like the new cook and stretch your comfort zone one **Iteration** at a time to fit your needs. Visualize your larger crust and carefully spin the dough until it's your desired size. Just for fun, count the **Iterations** from a ball of dough to a finished pizza on the pan.

Then **Celebrate** success with an excellent hot pizza—in the oven, not on the floor!

Practice As You Learn

Think of one area in which you need to expand your comfort zone. Create a mental vision and **Plan** of how you will enlarge your ability in that area.

Innovating Personal Change at Work

Change happens 24/7 in everything we do—work, family, personal, social, and community. When changes are required, we have two choices: (1) complain or (2) look forward to using the new method for change.

When you **Plan** a vacation, you are excited to go. You can also be enthused about change in the workplace.

This story is about creating an exciting new opportunity at work.

> ➜ *Emma was the office manager for a 45-person technology company. She told the CEO that she had always wanted to learn more about accounting, so he trained her to prepare customer invoices and track accounts receivable in QuickBooks®. A few weeks later, Emma mentioned attending an Accounting 101 class every Saturday through the university's continuing education program. She hoped that if she learned more independently, she would be allowed to help with more accounting for the company. The CEO loved her enthusiasm!*

*Not only did her **Innovative Plan** work to do the company's accounting, but they also reimbursed the tuition. Emma was excited as she accomplished her new vision of herself in the company and earned her reward.* ⬅

Practice As You Learn

Think about how you typically react to two different types of events:

- A change at work that is entirely beyond your control.
- A change that you initiate around one of your personal goals.

How do your feelings differ when you're driving the change? Why?

The Value of Innovation

Innovation is the lifeblood of everything.

- Organizations **Innovate** change to improve processes and products.
- Accountants love it when **Innovation** reduces cost, putting more profit on the bottom line.
- Ergonomists **Innovate** for improvements that put less stress on the body when moving or sitting.
- We all like it when **Innovation** brings more enjoyment to our activities or productivity.

Innovating the Mobile Device

If you are old enough, you may remember one of the original brick cell phones. They were called brick phones because they were heavy and looked like you were holding a brick up to your ear.

Motorola created the working prototype for a cellular phone in 1973, but it took the FTC 10 years to approve it for sale. The 2 lb. "brick" had a whopping 30-minute battery life!

Then, the **Innovation** race began. SMS texting was added, spurring dozens of companies to enter the market.

The first smartphone, "Simon," was the **Innovation** of IBM (Not Apple) in 1994, giving the phone a touchscreen, email, and a few built-in apps like a calculator.

Apple introduced the iPhone in 2007. A year later, HTC and Google introduced the HTC Dream Android phone, and the race between iOS and Android heated up. Did you know that Microsoft also developed a mobile operating system that quickly faded into the dust?

Today, hundreds of **Innovative Iterations** later, the cell phone has become a genuine mobile device that has changed the world.

> *Create once, then **Innovate** and **Iterate** before you (or your product) quickly become obsolete.*

VISION

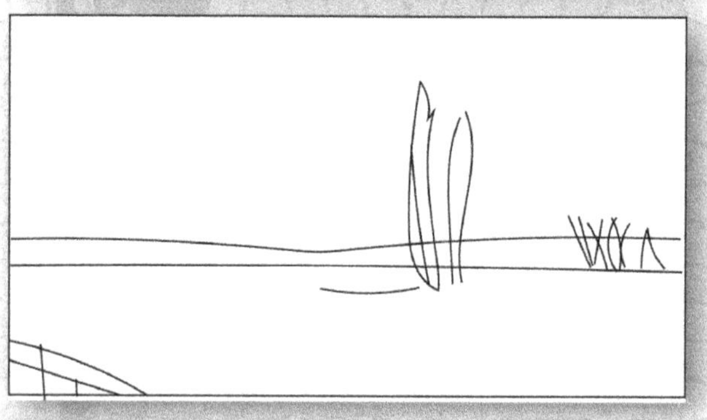

OUTLINE

INNOVATE

You can Learn to Create and Innovate

So many people say, "I'm not Creative or **Innovative**." They usually think of the visual or performing arts; even then, maybe they've never tried or were stifled. Learning to sketch or paint is a fun example that everyone can do.

Step 1: Start with a photograph of what you want to paint. A photo is easier than painting outdoors (called plein air).

Step 2: Take a piece of paper and draw a light pencil outline of the picture on the blank paper. Here's where a workshop, coach, or YouTube video will help you understand how to recreate the size, shapes, and proportions of your picture as you outline.

In "art" language, you are outlining to separate the positive and negative spaces.

Step 3: Finally, you add colors one at a time as you **Innovate** the style, shading, background, etc.

Your first sketch (or painting) probably won't turn out exactly as you wanted. Analyze what you would like to change and repaint it again as a new **Iteration**.

One artist-teacher half-jokingly predicts that you'll need to do 200-400 paintings until you can produce something you feel good about selling.

Practice As You Learn

Think of a product or organization that didn't **Innovate** fast enough and is no longer the industry leader or failed entirely. (Hint: Kodak, Polaroid.)

What could they have done to stay the leader in their field or still exist today?

Innovation Outside Work

We have discussed how the **Innovation** Habit can benefit an organization, product, or service, but what about your life?

What if you want to **Innovate** around your health (lose weight, run a marathon, have 6-pack abs), become a better parent (quality and quantity time, help with homework, be less critical), or learn something new (golf, piano, a hobby)?

We will discuss this later in Chapter 9 but think about how an **Innovation** mindset can be a powerful tool for improving your life and relationships.

Key Takeaways from this Chapter

- **Innovation** is necessary to be a leader in your work and personal life.
- Don't be afraid to color outside the lines.
- **Innovate** everything you do.
- Once you create, **Innovate** to keep it growing.

Final Practice As You Learn

Take a piece of paper and write five ways to sharpen a pencil. Were you **Innovative?**

Quick Quiz

> *Which of these statements are true about "Innovation?"*

True   False

O   O   Create something new.

O   O   Change something that exists.

O   O   Used during **Planning** a project.

O   O   Used when developing a solution to a problem.

**You innovate something that exists so the answer to "Create something new," is false. Think of yourself as an innovator in the last three statements.

> **Innovation makes each step of the Change Journey more successful---like compounding interest.**

10
8
9
7
5
6
4
2
3
1
START

Chapter 4

HABIT 4 - **PLAN** the Change

In Habit #2, you learned how to create an exciting **Vision** for your project. The **Vision** could be to solve a problem, improve, or pursue something you want to achieve personally—like learning to play an instrument.

The **Project Plan** is a roadmap that defines the **Iterations** required to achieve the **Vision**.

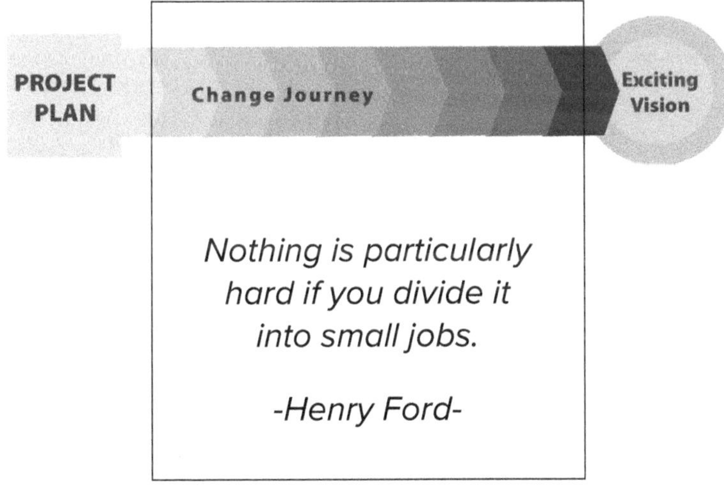

Four Requirements in a Simple Project Plan

Keep your **Project Plans** simple. You seldom need sophisticated project management software; spreadsheets will do the job just fine.

A good **Project Plan** should include four categories of details.

1)   **Required:**   Deadlines, budget, etc.

2)   **Activities:**   The tasks to achieve the **Vision**.

3)   **Optional:**   Bonus results when possible.

4)   **Celebrate:**   **Celebrate** success along the journey.

Preparing a Simple Project Plan

Project Planning for a Change Journey should be simple. Ignore the Gantt, PERT, RACI, and other complicated charts that few understand.

Collect the data using a piece of paper or a spreadsheet. Then, illustrate the **Plan** using a Word doc or spreadsheet or hand-draw a fun visual to share with the team. Remember: A written **Plan** has a better chance at success than a **Plan** in your head that the team can't see.

The following example illustrates how you gather data, organize it into incremental **Iterations**, and create a **Project Plan**.

Let's walk through the **Project Planning** for a fun vacation in Yellowstone.

Example of Planning a Trip to Yellowstone

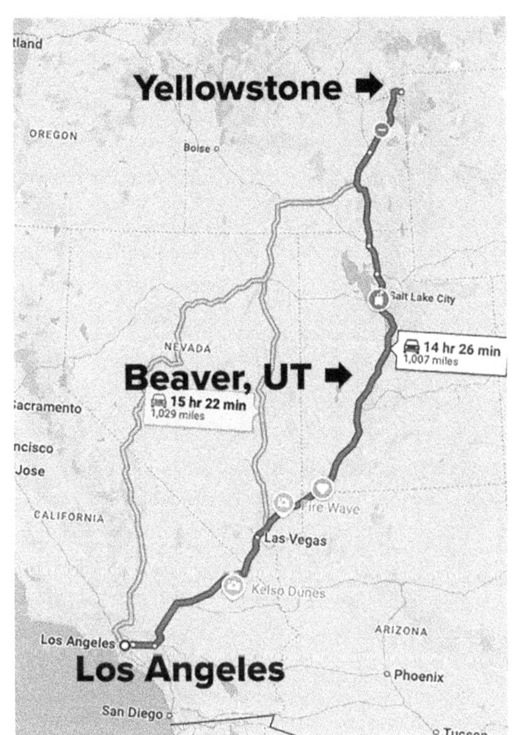

Suppose you want to take your family to Yellowstone National Park, and you live in Los Angeles.

At first glance, the route seems easy: Just jump on I-15, drive 17 hours (1,017 miles) straight through, and end up at your location like a zombie.

This is at least a two-day trip so you could stop halfway.

Beaver, Utah, is halfway, but it's a small town with only a couple of local motels and a handful of fast-food restaurants.

It's not exactly a vacation destination!

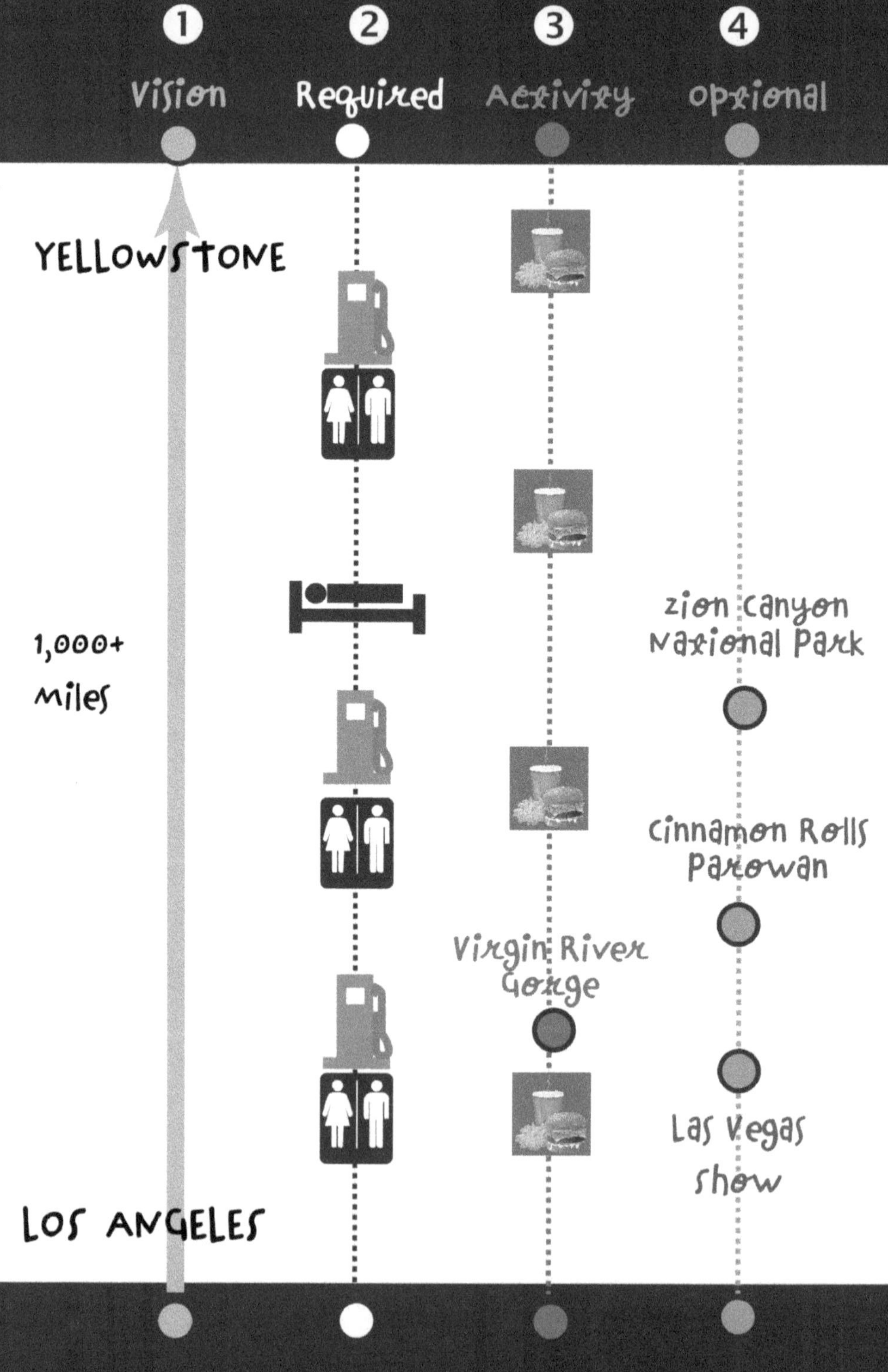
1
Vision
2
Required
3
Activity
4
Optional
YELLOWSTONE
1,000+
miles
zion Canyon
National Park
Cinnamon Rolls
Parowan
Virgin River
Gorge
Las Vegas
show
LOS ANGELES

Planning The 5 Habit Way

[1] Vision: Take a piece of paper and draw a line from Los Angeles (the starting point) at one end and "Yellowstone" (your **Vision**) at the other--- a long 1,017-mile drive.

Next, consider the factors affecting the trip and plot them on the line.

[2] Required: For this example, you'll need gas or charge for your car, so plan to stop every 300+ miles. The same for restroom breaks? Anything else required?

[3] Activity: Plan some stops for food and other along the way. Activity and Optional factors are where you can **Innovate**. Apply the "Things to Do" filter on your Google Maps and scroll through the route you'll take. You'll be amazed at the things to do as you drive by.

The I-15 freeway takes you through the spectacular Virgin River Gorge. Add that so the family can **Celebrate** it as a milestone.

[4] Optional: Are there any side trips you've always wanted to take? How about a show in Las Vegas or hiking in Zion Canyon National Park? These activities will slow the drive, but they make the journey more fun. Plot these optional factors on your line.

If you haven't already, this is a perfect time to bring in the family (team) and get their input. For example, someone may want to visit Snow Canyon instead of Zion Canyon or see Big Rock Candy Mountain!

YELLOWSTONE, WY

Day 3
363 miles
5.5 hr

Provo, UT

Day 2
377 miles
5 hr

Cinnamon Rolls
Parowan, UT

Zion Canyon
National Park

Virgin River
Gorge

Las Vegas, NV

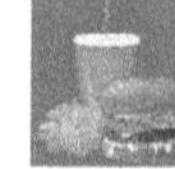

Las Vegas fun,
Dinner, Plus show

Day 1
271 miles
5 hr

LOS ANGELES, CA

Use the "What If" Technique

With the key factors plotted, let's **Innovate** and break this trip into realistic and enjoyable chunks. This is where the **"what if"** technique is valuable. You simply think **"what if"** I organized the required-activity-optional items into groups, then stand back and look at your **Plan**.

Then **Iterate** and ask again, **"what if"** I shuffled them differently. Soon you'll have several alternatives to choose from. This "what if" example is divided into three days.

WHAT IF: You allow five hours of driving daily, leaving five-plus hours for fun.

Day 1: Explore Las Vegas and take in a show at the Shelby Center and overnight in Las Vegas, Nevada.

Day 2: Drive through Virgin River Gorge, enjoy cinnamon rolls, and hike in Zion Canyon National Park. Overnight in Provo, Utah.

Day 3: Arrive at Yellowstone with plenty of leisure time

** Each night, you'll stay at a location with dozens of hotels and plenty of restaurants.

Celebrate: Each day leaves plenty of time for fun and gets you closer to Yellowstone.

Example of an Organizational Project Plan

Let's create a Project **Plan** to replace all the desktop computers in a company that has 100 computers. The **Vision** is to install new systems so everyone can enjoy faster computing that doesn't crash in the middle of a project.

Following the **Project Planning** method, here's the **Project Plan**.

Vision: Install new systems so everyone can enjoy faster computing without crashes.

Required: Replace 100 computers by the end of the month. Workers need their computers during the business day. The budget won't allow the IT team overtime to make the change after hours. Minimal amount of disruption for users.

Activity: Break the implementation into **Iterations** by department.

Optional: If possible, complete before the end of the month.

Celebrate: Bring doughnuts for everyone involved in that day's step and recognize the IT team for their hard work.

These are the eight **Iterations** in this **Project Plan**. Each **Iteration** is **Planned** to take one day:

1. Install Reception and Miscellaneous (5 computers)

2. Sales Department (15)

3. Accounting and administration (20)

4. Production (20)

5. Shipping (20)

6. Marketing and Operations (20)

7. Survey all departments to ensure satisfaction

8. Final **Celebration** – Take IT team to lunch

When the IT team started the Project, they found a need to **Innovate** some changes as they worked on the **Plan**. (You'll learn these tips and tricks in the next few chapters.)

Day 1: On the first day of installation, the IT team hauled boxes of desktops and monitors into the reception area and started to unpack. The receptionist wasn't happy about the mess in the beautiful lobby, and visitors were dodging boxes and packing. However, the IT team struggled through and finished the reception, conference room, and break room by the end of the day.

However, the feedback was intense, so they **Iterated** a revision for the next day.

Day 2: Today, they unpacked all the boxes in the warehouse and carried only the hardware to the salesroom. Things were less messy, but each salesperson complained that it took too long to install, run updates, and configure the computers—so long that the IT team could only change over half of the machines.

Feedback from day two was that it was taking too much time and interrupting sales.

Day 3: The IT team took a one-day "intermission" to **Innovate** a way to speed up each installation.

They created a "prep area" in a training room where they could unpack, install updates, and configurations while in the prep-training room instead of at the user's workstation.

Day 4: Using the newly **Iterated** process, each worker's downtime was minimal. They finished the sales area before noon. Sales were ecstatic about the improvement and the treat!

Day 5: Using the twice-**Iterated** process, they spent the morning unpacking and configuring, then installed 20 desktops in the accounting department during the afternoon. Today, the users are thrilled with the minimal interruption and the doughnuts.

Day 6+: With their process perfected, they completed the rest of the project ahead of schedule.

Oh, yes, the Project Manager took the IT team to a very nice lunch as a reward and **Celebration**.

Innovative Planning Tips

Broad Strokes:

Pre-**Plan** each step, but only in broad strokes. Expect a few bumps while discovering what worked and what didn't work for that step. Build some flexibility into the timeline. Then, **Iterate** and update the next step.

Learn from Mistakes:

Theodore Roosevelt said it all:

"The only man who never makes a mistake is the man who never does anything."

Include Your Team:

Include your team or at least representatives from the team in the **Planning**. They will be more motivated to work hard on something they have contributed to. They will also have insights you don't have as a project manager.

Include Stakeholders:

Ensure that all stakeholders agree. This will help you manage expectations when the unexpected occurs.

Celebrate:

Compliment and **Celebrate** small successes along the way. Even someone who didn't actively participate will eat the goodies you bring to **Celebrate**!

Key Takeaways from this Chapter

- **Project Plans** should be simple.
- Invite the implementation team to help with the **Planning**.
- Include: **Vision**, Required, Activities, Optional, and **Celebrate**.
- **Innovate** with some "What If" ideas.
- Share with all stakeholders to align expectations and receive feedback.

Final Practice As You Learn

Draw a project **Plan** using at least five logical "Activity" **Iterations** for hypothetically replacing your laptop or phone with a new one. Five **Iterations** might be overkill for accomplishing this simple **Vision** but accept the challenge for five anyway.

Quick Quiz

> *Which of these changes would be improved by creating a simple **Project Plan** with **Iterations**?*

[ ] Upgrading your car.

[ ] Building a doghouse.

[ ] Playing an online team game.

[ ] Going to a movie.

[ ] Creating a **Vision** Board.

[ ] A well-**Planned** vacation.

Every Change Journey benefits from a simple **Project Plan**. Thinking ahead helps you work faster and more effectively. And remember to celebrate your success.

The Project Plan is the roadmap to achieve your wonderful Vision.

Chapter 5

HABIT 5 - **CELEBRATE** Success

Celebrating helps people share their emotions, whether joy, happiness, or sorrow.

Practice As You Learn

Take a piece of paper and list at least 20 **Celebrations** you experienced or observed in the past year. (National, local, work, family, personal) How did each **Celebration** make you feel?

Create A Culture of Celebration

A **Celebration** is a positive expression of emotion. Why not spread "positive" regularly?

As participants, we **Celebrate** birthdays, marriages, holidays, new jobs, being on a winning sports team, and even hitting the jackpot in Las Vegas.

As observers, we **Celebrate** the Olympics, football, sports, graduations, award ceremonies, and even the inauguration of a new president.

We **Celebrate** even if the event is sorrowful--- **Celebrating** the life of a deceased person.

Do we forget to **Celebrate** at work or home, or are we too busy to stop and recognize a positive event?

A Change Journey is a perfect reason to **Celebrate** many times over!

Celebrating the Change Journey

This book illustrates many ways for your team to participate in an upcoming Change Journey. The team deserves to **Celebrate** a successful completion.

Along the way, incorporate "milestones" into your **Iterations** and share the milestone **Celebration** with everyone.

Even displaying a progress chart on the wall (or team site) helps everyone anticipate a successful completion.

Celebrating Each Iteration

Remember how an **Iteration** works?

Every time your team completes an **Iteration**, stop and have a little **Celebration**. If nothing else, a compliment or recognition in a team meeting.

Celebrating each **Iteration** might be focused on the people who performed the task, but if you build in some milestones, everyone can **Celebrate**.

Celebrate Failures Too

Researchers use **Iterations** to determine what doesn't work and help them discover what does. At the beginning of the journey, they may need to design a couple of **Iterations** to fine-tune the best approach to continue.

Other times, something unexpected interrupts the **Iteration**, and they **Innovate** a solution to continue the Journey.

Think of what you learn through failure as a positive and **Celebrate**!

Innovate Your Celebrations

Remember **Innovation** in your **Celebrations**. Be creative. Have some fun. Mix it up.

One Size Doesn't Fit All

Not everyone likes to **Celebrate** the same way. Know your people and remember that one size doesn't fit all.

Example #1: An office manager bought a stack of gift cards at the local coffeehouse. She would give out a gift card when she saw people going above and beyond or when she wanted to **Celebrate** a win. One day, while in Tom's office, she noticed that Tom had a pile of gift cards on his desk. When she asked, "Why haven't you used your gift cards?" Tom said, "Because I don't drink coffee."

Example #2: The founder of a company wanted to **Celebrate** the success that his little organization was having. While on a trip to New York City, he and his wife went into Tiffany's, bought every employee a very nice (expensive) Tiffany crystal bowl, and presented it to them as a thank you. What the founder didn't realize is that many of the employees in the office were struggling financially and would have appreciated a cash bonus instead. (Rather than having to go through the hassle of selling the bowl on E-bay.)

Key Takeaways from this Chapter

- People love to **Celebrate**.
- **Celebrate** every step of a Change Journey.
- **Celebrate** what you learned from mistakes and failures, too.
- Be creative and plan **Celebrations** that are meaningful.

Final Practice As You Learn

List at least 10 ways to **Celebrate** during or after your next Change Journey.

Self-Assessment

Rate yourself on a scale of 1-5 (1=low, 5=high)

1- I love to **Celebrate**.

1------2------3------4------5

2- I **Celebrate** each step of the Change Journey.

1------2------3------4------5

3- I look at failure or mistakes as positive.

1------2------3------4------5

5- My **Celebrations** are **Planned** and intentional.

1------2------3------4------5

* If you feel a need to raise any of your scores,
you know how to do it by now!

**Use the Celebrate Change Habit to make the
change Journey fun!**

Chapter 6

6 - Fine Tuning Results

You've been introduced to the 5 Simple Habits for Successful Change. The rest of this book shares tips that you can use for a change that you are working on today.

There are dozens of valuable techniques for Fine-Tuning your success. Many are easy and fun, while some are laborious and impractical. This chapter provides a few easy-to-do favorites.

The Role of ROI to Guide the Vision

You may be asked to make a significant change at work, leaving you to figure out how to make it happen. Here's how to get started:

- Create an exciting **Vision** of the desired end state after the **Innovation**.

- Create a project **Plan** by **Innovating** and **Iterating** on the path.

- Calculate the budget needed in dollars, human resources, and downtime. Remember to calculate the cost savings, efficiency, and value it will bring to the company and employees.

- The costs compared to value define the Return on Investment (ROI). Stakeholders always want to know the ROI!

There may be times when the ROI suggests you cancel the proposed change. Don't be afraid to speak up if the ROI doesn't justify the change.

There's Value in Doing Nothing

Here's a story to illustrate when it's OK to do nothing.

➜ *The professor of a business management class gave the students a hypothetical Human Resources problem to solve. Then, he left the classroom while students labored over a perfect solution. He returned 15 minutes later. One of the students presented their lengthy, extensive solution.*

The wise professor paused thoughtfully and said, "What if we did nothing?"

The students looked at each other and realized they had created a gigantic, impractical solution for an insignificant issue.

Lesson learned, professor! ⬅

As part of your **Innovation**, don't be afraid to discard ideas even if they seem great! We lost count of the ideas we threw out when writing this book!

Perfect Practice, Not Practice Makes Perfect

Think about how we master a new skill. We practice (**Iterate**) repeatedly, hoping that our skills improve.

You've probably heard this before: "Practice doesn't make perfect". Only "perfect practice makes improvement." This quote points out that repeating the same thing repeatedly requires a process for improvement to lead to success.

Unless we do something to improve each **Iteration**, we will not grow. That's why great athletes have a coach, musicians have a teacher, etc. The coach or teacher tells them how to improve their next practice **Iteration.**

Most of the time, you won't have a coach. Instead, you **Innovate** yourself as to what you will do differently during the next **Iteration**.

The Importance of Feedback with Each Iteration

Feedback is essential for driving successful **Innovation** and guiding the next **Iteration**. Feedback methods range from sophisticated systems to simple conversations with a trusted person.

Most companies have real-time data available for decision-making.

Here's a story about how instant feedback helped the owners quickly **Innovate** a solution to a problem.

> ➜ *Benito and Sofia own three franchises of a popular cookie store. Their software provides real-time reports they review at the end of each day.*
>
> *On a Tuesday night, they noticed that one of the store's chocolate chip cookie sales was almost zero that day. (Chocolate chip cookies are one of the top sellers.)*
>
> *The following day, they met with the manager, who was new, and discovered that they had forgotten to order chocolate chips in the weekly supply order. The store had run out. Benito worked with the new manager to understand the reordering process while Sofia drove to a nearby grocery store to buy chocolate chips.*
>
> *They solved a temporary problem and got the store back on track because of daily feedback.* ⬅

Benito and Sofia were rewarded for their efforts by bringing the profit back to par, and they also enjoyed a freshly baked chocolate chip cookie.

Take An Intermission

Sometimes, we get so immersed in innovating and **Iterating** that we "can't see the forest for the trees." That's when stepping back—taking a deliberate intermission—can make all the difference.

The book "Juggling Elephants" (Todd Musig and Jones Loflin) emphasizes the power of intermissions to recharge and refocus.

An intermission doesn't have to be extravagant. It could be a 15-minute walk, an hour-long lunch with friends, or even a day off to reset your perspective.

The value lies in returning refreshed—physically, mentally, and emotionally. It's about giving yourself space to stretch, reflect, and gain clarity so you're sharper and more effective when you dive back in.

As Leonardo da Vinci wisely said:

"Now and then, go away, relax, for when you return to work, your judgment will be surer."

Take a pause. Your work and your well-being will thank you.

> *Consider assigning an Intermission as one of the Iterations in a lengthy Project **Plan**.*
> *Or take an intermission when something unexpected appears that needs time to **Innovate**.*

Fake Music

Chords
Melody
Eb maj7
Dm7
Cm7
Bb maj7
Dm7
Em7
Fmaj7
Bm7
Dm7
Em7
Fmaj7
Fo7
Em7
Dm7
C maj7
Bm7

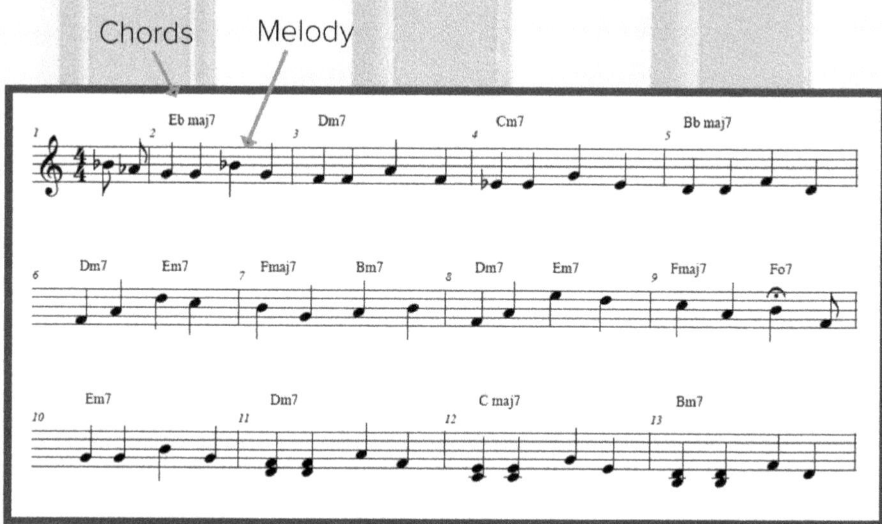

Each Iteration Accomplishes Something New

Each iteration should test or add something new towards your **Vision** and not repeat itself. Consider this story as told by a piano student.

> ➜ *I wanted to learn to play the piano using the "fake music" style. This is where the written music is a simple melody with notations for chords above. Most bands play using fake music, allowing the musicians to improvise as they play.*
>
> ***Iteration 1*** *My teacher started me with the MAJOR seventh chords. It took a couple of weeks to get comfortable playing these chords from "muscle memory." The practice songs were simple and blah, with only MAJOR chords in my skillset.*
>
> ***Iteration 2*** *The next **Iteration** was to learn the MINOR cords. Practice songs became more enjoyable when using MAJOR and MINOR chords.*
>
> ***Iteration 3*** *The third **Iteration** focused on the DOMINANT seventh cords. Now, I could play with three chord types, and the songs became music!*
>
> *Every **Iteration** taught me something new while building upon what I learned in the previous **Iteration**.* ⬅

Each **Iteration** should move onto something new instead of repeating the same thing.

An Example of a Small Change with Big Results

Look at this credit card number, for example. Comprehending or reciting the 16 digits is challenging and prone to errors---like a Change Journey with one **Iteration**!

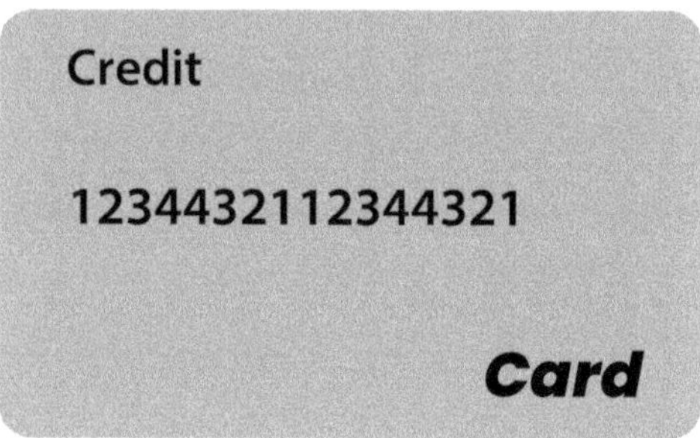

Now, look at the same number divided into four pieces---Like a Change Journey with **Iterations**.

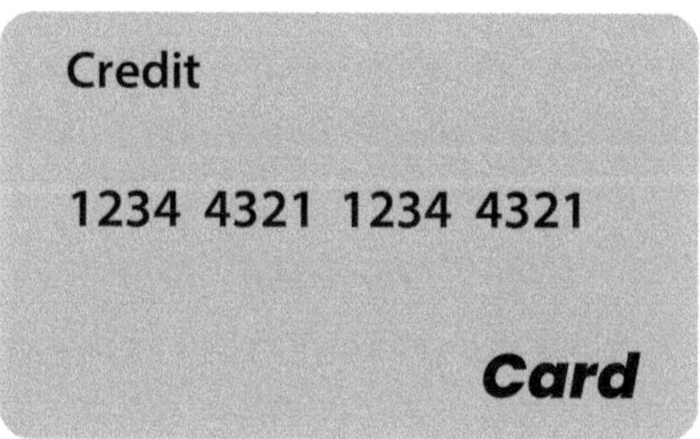

- Is the number more straightforward to comprehend now?

- Can you see the patterns the numbers make? Did you see the patterns without the spaces?

- Is it easier to speak the number to someone?

Progress is What You Make It

Enjoy this story about a positive attitude towards change.

> ➔ *A manufacturing worker, Janice, practiced and worked hard to be the best operator of a specialized machine. She knew every nuance of the machine and of the software driving it.*
>
> *Management changed the software a few months after Janice had received an award for being the plant's top machine operator. She was overwhelmed because she worked hard to become the best with the existing software.*
>
> *As her manager, how could you help Janice and others through this change that is beyond their control?*
>
> *Janice acknowledged that the change would happen and could not stop it. Then, she remembered attending a training class on the "5 Simple Habits for Successful Change."*
>
> *So, she **Innovated** an aggressive **Vision** and set a three-day deadline for herself to make the change. She **Planned** precisely what she wanted to accomplish each day (iterations). As a result, she mastered the latest software in just three days.*
>
> *Her manager noticed her willing attitude and fast adoption of the new software and recommended that she become the implementation trainer for other plants facing the exact software change.* ⬅

She enjoyed both the travel and the bump in pay.

Key Takeaways from this Chapter

- Sometimes, there is value in doing nothing.
- Share the value of the **Vision**.
- Perfect practice, not practice Makes perfect.
- Use feedback from each **Iteration** to improve the next **Iteration**.
- Remember the importance of intermissions.
- Each **Iteration** should accomplish something new.
- Expand your comfort zone through change.
- Progress is what you make of it.

Final Practice As You Learn

Fix something special for dinner tonight. Then, fix the same menu tomorrow night, but **Iterate/Innovate** and enhance the experience. Use different spices or ingredients. Change the presentation if nothing else.

After you serve it, ask the person who ate it or ask yourself, "If I were running a restaurant, is this good enough to go on the menu?"

Quick Quiz

Answer these true/false questions.

True False Question

O   O   **Iterating** well-designed steps will improve results.

O   O   If I practice long enough, I will get it perfect.

O   O   I should repeat the same actions during each **Iteration** because things will change automatically.

O   O   Feedback improves the next **Iteration**.

O   O   It's better to be like a bull in a China shop than to **Iterate** my progress in small steps.

Answers: T, F, F, T, F

Iteration and **Innovation** can add security when making a change.

Chapter 7

7 - Pulling a Team Together

Teams can be as small as one person or the 40,000 laborers who built the pyramids in Egypt.

Although the logistical challenges vary, involving the team in the 5 Simple Habits for Change will make the journey fun, fast, and effective.

Later in this chapter, we'll discuss applying this new mindset across different organizational structures.

Who are the Stakeholders?

A stakeholder is anyone interested in making an organization, team, project, or task successful. Investors have a vested financial interest but are usually uninvolved in day-to-day operations.

How do you identify the stakeholders?

- Who has a financial stake in the project?
- Who will be directly or indirectly impacted?
- Who influences the project's success or failure?
- Who has authority, resources, or knowledge?

The Team

Change may be initiated at any organizational level. This graphic illustrates typical stakeholder roles.

Champion: The person with the authority and budget to authorize a change.

Planning Team: A project manager and assistants who organize and direct the change project.

Doer: These people perform the activity required to make the change.

Influencer: People who are directly affected by the change. This group can make or break the project, so be sure to involve them in whatever way appropriate.

Observer: The change will affect these people, but they don't care. These may be part-time or contract employees with no long-term **Vision** for employment or vendors.

Don't shut out the observers. They may have good ideas and feedback.

The CEO or stockholders may be observers or champions. Either way, be sure to listen carefully to their expectations!

Risk, Innovation, and Limiting Factors

This graphic illustrates how Risk, **Innovators,** and Limiters relate to the Roles.

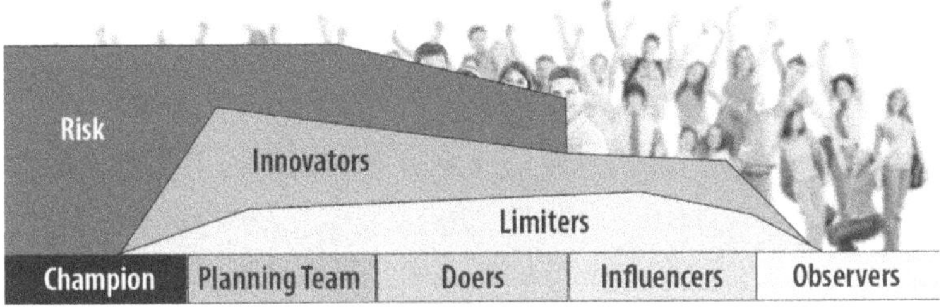

Risk: The Champion assumes the primary risk for a change project, but the planning team and doers may receive some of the fallout if it goes awry.

Innovators and Limiters : The Planning Team should always consider the **Innovations** and limitations expressed by the Doers and the Influencers. If the project fails, they will be the biggest complainers.

Creating Team Buy-in

The best way to create "Buy-In" is by letting people be involved in their destinies.

(1) When everyone participates and shares in creating the **Vision** of a beautiful new state, they are all in.

(2) Plus, when their **Innovations** and cautions are incorporated into the **Project Plan**, they will do all they can to support the project's success.

*PS: They will also enjoy **Celebrating** when it's complete.*

What About Vendors?

Vendors are often overlooked when trying to improve an organization's process. As this story illustrates, vendors can be a great source of **Innovation** on your behalf.

➜ *A marketing specialist was responsible for running extensive direct mail campaigns and had developed a good working relationship with a particular printer. He liked this small vendor's responsiveness and excellent customer service.*

One day, the vendor asked for a meeting to share an idea. The vendor had watched the company's inefficiency when applying address labels by hand to the mail pieces. The vendor offered to take over addressing the mail pieces via automation at a slight increase in cost.

The company's approval allowed the vendor to purchase the automated labeling equipment to speed up production time. It became a win-win for everyone. ⬅

Large Organizations

Change Projects across large organizations can be more challenging. One large organization spread across three nearby buildings solved it this way.

> ➜ *A healthcare organization was required to create a HIPAA compliance committee to manage the changes required to improve the company's HIPAA compliance.*
>
> *A representative from each department in each of the three buildings was assigned to the committee. The department heads were told to find representatives from the front-line workers. No department heads allowed!*
>
> *Each person enthusiastically accepted the responsibility. They were empowered to speak on behalf of their co-workers. In their local department meetings, they gathered ideas and supervised assignments.*
>
> *Since the buildings were within a few miles of each other, the representatives looked forward to "getting out of the office" for committee meetings.*
>
> *Through the committee structure, the project lead could delegate the training and implementation of the HIPAA privacy changes in their respective departments through the representatives.* ⬅

The secret to successful organizational change is to **Innovate** ways to share the **Vision** and allow everyone to give feedback on the project.

Generating and Sustaining Motivation

The definition of Inertia from Dictionary.com states:

A property of matter where it continues in its existing state of rest or uniform motion in a straight line unless an external force changes that state.

Once the first **Iteration** rolls, it will continue with inertia unless your team loses interest and grinds to a halt, like gravity or friction.

Remember the Slinky? It keeps moving forward on its own.

Riding a bicycle requires forward motion to stay in balance. What happens when you stop? It takes effort to start again, so don't let your project stop until it is finished.

An airplane requires air to move constantly across the wing to create lift. A gusty wind isn't enough to raise the plane off the runway. Massive engines generate a constant thrust, pushing the plane forward and creating lift on the wings.

➔ *Remember when the plane taking off from LaGuardia airport hit a flock of birds, destroying both engines? The skilled pilot had less than three minutes to land safely on the only clear space available - the Hudson River.* ⬅

Like the pilot, quickly address any conflict that arises so you can make a safe landing.

If you are leading the change project, find **Innovative** ways to motivate the team throughout the project, not just at the beginning. Let the team tell you what they need to stay enthused. Do they want doughnuts or bagels?

Remote Teams

Remote teams became an instant norm during COVID. Today, many teams still work remotely.

Yet remote teams still need to collaborate. Most teams still have regular meetings on Zoom, Microsoft Teams, Google Workspace, or other platforms. Just like in-person meetings, these occasions can be used to create and share the **Vision**, **Innovate**, and obtain buy-in. Just follow the tips throughout this book.

Online workspaces usually have a splash screen for announcements. On that screen, post a picture of the **Vision** and a graphic showing progress.

Key Takeaways from this Chapter

- Use the roles of each team member to assess how to put them to work.
- Recruit cheerleaders.
- Keep momentum and watch for friction or stalls.
- There are **Innovative** ways to include every team member in every organizational structure. (In-person, remote, mixed, multi-location.)

Final Practice As You Learn

Analyze your department and decide which people would be a great asset when implementing the required change.

Who would understand the limiting factors? Who would expand your thinking with **Innovative** optional/bonus ideas?

Who will be your cheerleaders?

Quick Quiz

> *Which of these could get more people involved in the change process?*

[ ] Create a change committee with representatives from each area.

[ ] Invite **Innovative** ideas from everyone involved in the change process.

[ ] Create a dynamic **Vision** with several of your colleagues.

[ ] Creating a **Vision** board or scoreboard.

[ ] Celebrate as a team at the end of each **Iteration**.

**All of these ideas get more people involved.

Involving a team will make a change project more successful!

Chapter 8

8 - Coaching the Winning Team

While this book focuses on organizations, remember that this mindset applies to family, friends, social groups, and the community. Have you noticed that most community meetings end in descent, mistrust, and conflict when **Innovation** and collaboration could smooth the ruffled feathers?

Encourage Spontaneous Participation

How many "suggestion" boxes have you seen empty? Or the suggestions disappear into an astronomical black hole. Soon, lunchtime conversations focus on what's wrong rather than what could be done.

Everyone should be taught the 5 Habits concept and invited to share their **Visions** for improvement that would benefit the organization at any level.

Integrate 5 Simple Habits for Successful Change in Your Culture

Teach the 5 Habits to your team. Here's where your leading by example will speak louder than your words.

Try your new mindset the next time you hand out a new assignment.

5 Simple Habits for Successful Change

1-Iterate

Use the "What If" technique to organize the data into logical **Iterations**. Evaluate progress and feedback after each **Iteration** and adjust the next **Iteration** to be more effective and stay on course.

2-Vision

Invite the team to help you turn the goal into a **Vision**. Remember to focus on the benefits. Think about a fun or novel way to introduce the assignment. Bring chips and salsa. Maybe start with the 5 Whys of how this assignment brings value to the company. (Or family, or social group, etc.)

3-Innovate

Encourage everyone to **Innovate** as they work on the project. **Innovation** increases motivation as each team member takes ownership of their task and the outcome.

4-Project Plan

Get the team involved to gather data on

(1) Requirements, (2) Activities (3) Optional

5-Celebrate

Reward the efforts of everyone involved.

Feedback - Learn Faster

Thomas Edison was determined to create a light bulb that worked. After hundreds of **Iterations**, his team found that tungsten would be a good material to make the filament for the bulbs. His team kept track of all the failed materials so they wouldn't waste time repeating a material known to fail.

When they settled on Tungsten, they continued to **Iterate** with more experiments to perfect the bulb until it could be manufactured and sold.

Don't **Plan** on failing like Edison on each **Iteration** but do expect to learn something that can be used to improve the next **Iteration**.

Even if an **Iteration** went OK, ask your team, "How could we make the next **Iteration** even better?" If you can't think of a way to improve, think back to the story of "Five Whys" and ask yourself the question five times.

Getting the Team Involved

The story on the right illustrates an **Innovative** approach to getting the team involved and motivated.

>
>
>
>
>
>
>
>

Remember, each team member knows the requirements of their job and can contribute **Innovative** solutions. They can be your best resources when creating a Change Journey!

➜ An ***Innovative*** *business consultant was hired to work with a small company. The problem was that the team was confused about the overall company process. The right hand didn't know what the left hand was doing.*

The consultant wrapped the lunchroom walls in a company-wide meeting with a roll of butcher paper. The paper was divided into departments according to the company workflow, and a representative of each department drew a flow chart of that department's workflow.

The team was instructed to examine these drawings over the next two weeks. Whenever they had an idea to improve the workflow of any department, they wrote it on a Post-it sticky note and stuck it on the flowcharts.

When the consultant returned in two weeks, the walls were surprisingly covered with dozens of sticky notes placed by the team, which opened the door to improvements at every level.

*The **Innovative** team created a new **Vision** of the company's potential. Then, work began, **Iterating** the steps toward that **Vision**.* ⬅

Recruit Each Team Member to be an Innovator

When you receive an assignment to implement a change, you probably stay up late trying to figure out how to "talk" your team into mindlessly following.

Instead, get help—not from your therapist but from your team. They probably know the processes that need to be changed better than you.

Recruit them to help create a **Vision** and **Plan** the **Iterations** from day one. Let them be the **Innovators**. If you work together as a team from the start, you'll be amazed at how smoothly the project will be accomplished.

Your primary job will be to share the **Vision** and clear the path with the stakeholders so there are no surprises.

Innovating in an Existing Environment

➜ *In the 1990s a US Army supply depot desperately needed improvements. It was built in 1941 during World War II and still ran the same way, with the same equipment.*

So, the base commander decided to enlist the workers' ideas on how to improve efficiency. After all, who knew the equipment and processes better than the workers themselves?

*To encourage **Innovation**, a 2% reward, calculated for the first-year cost savings, was offered for any idea that saved money.*

*The ideas started rolling in. A $10,000 savings idea earned a $200 reward. Soon, ideas saved $50,000, with a $1,000 bonus paid to an **Innovative** worker. The momentum rolled on until **Innovation** was the main topic of discussion during lunch and breaks. Then, an idea emerged, resulting in a $2.5 million first-year savings!*

*Encouraging employee **Innovation** saved money and changed the culture from status quo to exciting.* ⬅

Before you bring in an outside efficiency consultant, empower and incentivize your own team to be **Innovators**.

Have Empathy for Your Team's Values

Each member of your team has different values. Some reserve Saturday or Sunday to attend church with their families, while others get up early to run or work out. Some get more done around people, while others prefer isolation and quiet.

Some have family, religious, or community obligations outside work, and some work a second job to make ends meet. Some love alcoholic drinks. Others don't drink alcohol or are in Recovery. Some are OK working in the "gray" areas. Others won't consider anything in the gray.

Achieving a successful **Vision** requires accepting all team members' values. **Iterate** on the concepts until you agree on value-positive solutions.

Value-Aligned Success

➡ *Patina was the top inside salesperson and loved making outbound cold calls. Management implemented a new high-pressure outbound sales process that made Patina uncomfortable because it stretched some of her values.*

She asked to keep using her proven successful methods but was told she needed to use the new process. As a result, her sales plummeted as she struggled to perform actions contrary to her values.

She decided to change companies and immediately succeeded in the new company, using methods that aligned with her values. ⬅

Patina chose to change jobs rather than stretch her values. The company lost a top employee when it refused to acknowledge her values.

Compliment "People." Correct "Behavior."

Everyone loves compliments, and nobody likes to be criticized for their actions. Problems and mistakes are caused by incorrect behavior, not bad people.

The next time you need to correct someone, discuss the mistake as "inadvertently made" and help them understand the issue so they won't repeat it.

Now, how do **Iteration** and **Innovation** help you? When you must address someone's poor behavior, be **Innovative**. Start by complimenting the person's good work before you confront their behavior. Make it clear that they do a great job; only a behavior needs correction.

The second time, **Innovate** yourself and improve your delivery of the corrective conversation.

Soon, you'll be able to handle the most challenging discussions without offending.

Overcoming the Peter Principle

Laurence J. Peter developed the Peter Principle after observing people who rose to a "level of incompetence" as they moved up in a management hierarchy.

His studies found that many people struggled with continued promotions to higher responsibilities until they were no longer effective and became "incompetent" to perform the new promotion. Consider this story.

> ➜ *Abby started working part-time at a fast-food restaurant while in college. It was fun work, and the company offered educational benefits. The franchise owner noticed she caught on fast and worked well with the other workers.*
>
> *Abby was rewarded with a promotion to shift supervisor with a bump in pay. The evening shift allowed her to continue taking day classes, so all was well for Abby.*
>
> *When she stopped for summer break, the owner asked if she wanted to become a store manager. She was delighted with the position and the increased pay, but soon, all was not well.*
>
> *Abby struggled to organize the shift schedule for 50 people, most of whom were part-time workers. She tried hard to keep everyone happy. Then she discovered that the fast-food industry is transient, and she needed to screen and hire new people every week. Whenever someone left, she felt the turnover was her fault as a poor manager.*

*She realized that being the store manager
required supervisory skills, inventory control, and
productivity goals that she didn't have yet. The
owner patiently coached her, but she had reached
a level of "incompetence" at the job. She asked if
she could return to being a shift supervisor. After
resuming her previous position, she was happy and
comfortable again.* ←

Did Abby reach her level of "incompetence," or did she fail at "change," or was her promotion "premature?"

Remember that the Peter Principle is based on historical results---assuming that history predicts the future.

Now that you know the 5 Habits for Change technique, can you change the future and avoid the "incompetence" scenario? Will a clear **Vision** and careful **Itcrations** change the future?

No one is expected to have all the local knowledge and skills required for a promotion position.

If you are in management, don't expect someone recently promoted to a new job to be fully competent on day one. Instead, work with the person to develop a progress **Plan** using the 5 Habits for Change method, helping them grow into the position.

If your organization has formal Leadership Development Programs, use them! If you don't have a formal program, invest in online programs to fill the gap for your newly promoted employees.

Key Takeaways from this Chapter

- Develop a Change Journey culture.
- Encourage spontaneous **Visioning**.
- Feedback helps you learn faster.
- Encourage and incentivize the team to be **Innovators**.
- Have empathy for team members' values.
- Compliment people--correct poor behaviors.
- Help team members overcome potential incompetence.
- Work with team members to grow into new roles.

Final Practice As You Learn

Identify a person with underperforming potential and **Innovate** a way to coach them toward success.

Self-Assessment

On a scale of 1-5 (1=low, 5=high) rate yourself on these questions.

1- I look at times of change as an opportunity to make the change a "team project" instead of "my project."

1------2------3------4------5

2- I recognize bad behavior rather than the person being bad.

1------2------3------4------5

3- I leverage the talent of others and collaborate when working on a change project.

1------2------3------4------5

4- I am empathetic and consider other people's values when interacting with them.

1------2------3------4------5

** If you feel a need to raise any of your scores, you know how to do it by now!

Use the 5 Simple Habits for Change at work and in everything you do.

Chapter 9

9 - Life Outside Work

If you feel that you spend all your time looking in the rearview mirror, you may need help looking forward—not only one day at a time but, next month, next year, or for your lifetime.

By now, you understand the 5 Simple Habits for Successful Change at work. This chapter will focus on your life outside work.

Supercharge Your Thinking

There are many factors to consider, including family, career, and social. The 5 Habits can supercharge your thinking:

1-Iterate: Take one of your personal **Visions** (goals) and break the work into smaller, more doable **Iterations**.

2-Vision: You already have some personal or family goals that you want to accomplish. Return to Chapter 2 and use the **Vision** method to turn your goals into beautiful **Visions**.

3-Innovate: Look at Chapter 3 and apply **Innovation** to your life outside work.

4-Project Plan: Check out Chapter 4 for ideas on creating a simple project plan to achieve your **Vision** for your self or your relationships.

5-Celebrate: Celebrate everything, even personal failure. Use the ideas in Chapter 5 to trigger your creativity.

Vision Your Entire Life

Have you ever tried to imagine what the rest of your life will be like? What do you really want from this life? Whether you're 8 or 88, the rest of your life is still in front of you. You have the power to make it whatever you want.

Let **"Visioning"** be your guide. You may want to break your life into segments and create a **Vision** for each segment. Each segment then gives you a stepping stone upwards onto the next segment.

Chapter 2 discussed creating a **Vision**. The real point here is that you don't need to buy into anyone else's dream. You create your own dream. Turn it into your **Vision**, then make it your reality.

Changing Behaviors

When you do something senseless, it doesn't mean you are bad. It just means that your behavior was inappropriate. So, how do you change behaviors?

If you want to get academic, you can Google "Social Cognitive Theory," "Theory of Planned Behavior," or "Transtheoretical Model."

These are common points to consider:

- Readiness to Change
- Barriers to Change
- Likelihood of Relapse
- Motivation

Or, easier yet, update your mindset to the 5 Simple Habits for Successful Change.

Sustaining Motivation

Look at the example of a Slinky® moving down a set of stairs. It moves with a fascinating inertia it generates internally. How can you develop that same kind of motivation within yourself? What habits can you put in place that will keep you moving forward?

It all starts with a clear **Vision** or picture of your future state. You can make it happen by picturing $10,000 in a savings account or a new certification you want to earn posted on your **Vision** board (bathroom mirror, refrigerator, office wall, etc.).

Even though the **Vision** might be two years away, **Iteration** will give you the regular small win to reward yourself for your progress.

For instance, a two-year **Vision** of $10,000 in savings broken into one-month **Iterations**.

Wouldn't you prefer to **Celebrate** 24 times as you watch your savings grow rather than get discouraged and give up? 24 **Celebrations** are motivational!

Practice As You Learn

How would you reward yourself 24 times for each small win?

Running To or Running From?

Let's pretend that you are RUNNING FROM a house that is on fire. Your running is based on fear, and except to get you to safety, you have no direction. You are reacting to something that has already happened. Running From is like looking in the rearview mirror and not watching the road ahead.

RUNNING TO is based on inspiration and is rewarding. Running To requires a clear **Vision** picture of where you are going and what you want to accomplish. If you aren't RUNNING TO a **Vision**, then you are RUNNING FROM your old state by default.

Here's something to think about. Firefighters are RUNNING TO the burning house. Why do they do that?

Practice As You Learn

Identify one or two habits or activities that you are "running from?" Then, using the "5 Habits," **Plan** how you'll change them to "running to."

Life Changing Events

Current Job: Your current job will be much more rewarding if you adopt an attitude of continuous learning and adopt the new mindset this book discusses.

Promotions: Before applying for a promotion, stretch your comfort zone and add the skills needed for the new position.

Career Change: Changing to a new company could be scary. But if you use your new mindset, you'll be successful. To be ready, you may need to develop new skills or refresh old skills. You may also need to stretch your comfort zone as you apply and interview with recruiters.

Marriage / Commitment: Developing a primary relationship takes work. Most of us engage in many **Iterations** of meeting people, searching for a special person we can trust and love. Keeping that special feeling alive will require a shared **Vision** you develop together. Work together as you **Iterate** the **Plan** and **Innovate** your lives.

Family: Create a **Vision** for strengthening or rebuilding relationships with your parents and siblings. Also, create a **Vision** featuring your own family (partner and kids). You already know how to create Change Journies for each **Vision**.

Death: All of us will be affected by someone close passing away. Today is a good time to begin planning how you will deal with these events.

Is a Career Reset on the Horizon?

You may decide to or need to reset your career at some point. This may be to increase your income, fulfill a lifelong desire, or adjust to a change in the marketplace.

This is where a clear **Vision** is most important. Ensure the **Vision** is practical and considers the need to make a living and enjoy what you enjoy. It may require additional schooling (each class is a new **Iteration**), which takes time. Fortunately, online learning allows more flexibility in scheduling, saves travel time, and accelerates learning with a self-paced curriculum.

You always have a choice with the 5 Habits mindset!

A Time to Be Realistic

Two reasons that "New Year's Resolutions" fail are that people (1) make too many and (2) bite off more than they can chew.

Focus is important. While you may have a long list of personal **Visions**, use the 5 Habits for Change techniques to create a Master **Project Plan**. The Master **Plan** will help you decide the priority and order in which to work on your **Visions**.

Your time and effort will be more effective working on your **Projects** systematically and/or sequentially than picking ten **Projects** that never get done.

Plus, working sequentially gives you many more reasons to **Celebrate**.

If you want

to use the

5 Simple Habits for Successful Change

process to

improve

your life

outside of work,

where

would you

start?

Five Areas of Your Life

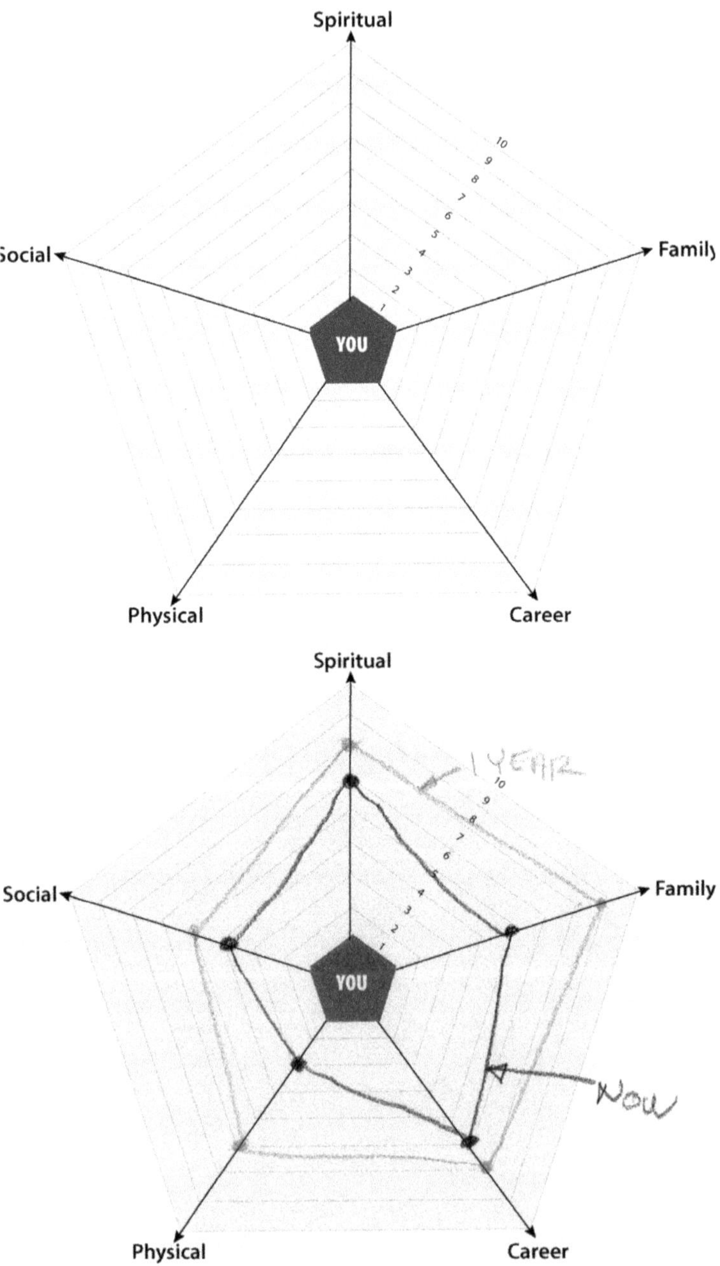

Areas of Your Life Exercise

If you wanted to use the 5 Habits for Change process to improve your life outside of work, where would you start?

The following enjoyable exercise identifies five aspects of your life to reflect on:

- Spiritual (self, religion, mental health)
- Family (significant other, children, parents)
- Social (friends, neighbors, social groups)
- Physical (health, physical activity)
- Career (school, profession, career change)

Start by rating yourself using the spider web chart.

- Rate yourself and mark a dot on the spoke line for each area.
- Then, connect the dots with your pencil. Does the graph look like a lumpy tire? There is no right or wrong. The graphic only shows how you rate things today.
- Next, using a different color, rate every spoke with where you would like to be in one year. Connect the dots again.
- Now, write a **Vision** for each of the future dots.
- Finally, pick one **Vision,** create a Project **Plan**, and start your journey.

Practice as You Learn

Make a copy of this page and do the Five Areas exercise.

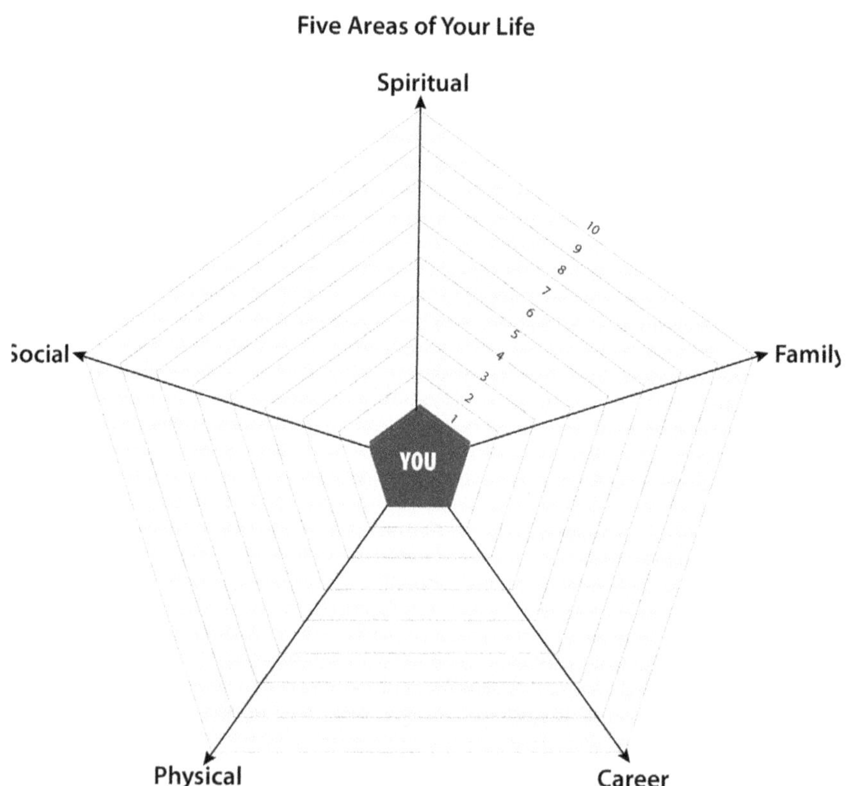

Your Lumpy Wheel

Your lumpy wheel will never become perfectly round. You must determine where you spend your time and what you want your future to become. Remember to be realistic and prioritize the order in which you will work on your **Visions.**

A blank PDF of this exercise is also available for download at www.5HabitsForChange.com.

Key Takeaways from this Chapter

- Create **Visions** for different stages of your life.
- Use the 5 Habits for Change to correct poor behaviors.
- Figure out how to sustain your motivation.
- Identify what are you Running To or Running From?
- Analyze the five areas of your life and where you want to be one year from now .
- Remember not to overwhelm yourself. Prioritize and order your **Visions**.

Final Practice As You Learn

Identify a small behavior change that you would like to make. Create a **Vision**, then a **Project Plan** with three short activity **Iterations**. Then **Plan** to **Celebrate** three small wins plus your final success!

Self-Assessment

> *On a scale of 1-5 (1=low, 5=high) rate yourself on these questions.*

1-I always achieve my New Year's resolutions.

1------2------3------4------5

2- I am "Running To" change, not "Running From" change in my life.

1------2------3------4------5

3- I have a clear **Vision** of my future.

1------2------3------4------5

4-I look for areas in my life that need improvement.

1------2------3------4------5

** If you feel a need to raise any of your scores, you know how to do it by now!

> **You won't know if you get there---if you don't know where you're going.**

-Dr. Wayne Dyer-
If you change
the way you look
at things,
the things you look at
change.

Chapter 10

10 - 5 Habits for Change in a Rapidly Changing World

In a world where markets shift by the minute, even the best-laid **Plans** can quickly go awry. You ask, "How do we keep up without losing footing?" The 5 Habits Mindset doesn't just help you adapt—it empowers you to thrive.

Creating Learning Environments

Encouraging a culture of sustainable learning means removing the fear of failure. People need "psychological safety"—the freedom to take risks and ask questions without fear of embarrassment or punishment. In an **Iterative** workplace, or in a family, psychological safety is built in. People feel comfortable exploring new approaches and sharing their insights. They **Celebrate** the journey, not just the outcome.

Teams with an **Iterative** and **Innovative** mindset become experts at breaking down complex challenges into small steps that lead to successful change.

Adapting the 5 Habits for Change

Adobe navigated a significant industry shift, transitioning from selling boxed software to a subscription model.

Their **Vision** was to convince users that their subscription model offered a better value-added product and was not a loyalty penalty.

> ➡ *To overcome resistance to the pricey subscription model, Adobe bundled over twenty different software programs into the new Creative Cloud bundle. A typical user seldom uses more than two or three of the programs but getting a bundle of 20+ increases the perceived value of the subscription.*
>
> *Then AI became a reality, and Adobe created a new **Vision** of being a leader in AI. They wanted to wow users, and the secret sauce was "**Iteration**" again.*
>
> *In the past, software companies were infamous for releasing beta programs to techies and asking them to help debug them. Mainstream users stayed away from beta versions to avoid disrupting their work.*
>
> *Adobe's "Beta" program for Photoshop and Illustrator in 2024 was **Innovative**. Adobe provided a proven version as a beta version with all of the previous functionality intact. Then, they carefully **Iterated** AI enhancements in the software over time. Users were excited to try*

the next AI features as they were incrementally introduced.

Users accepted minor bugs in a new AI feature, knowing it would be quickly fixed and enhanced. The "New Update Available" notice became something to look forward to instead of "oh no." Users became de facto members of the design and testing process and loved it! ←

Today, Adobe is a world leader in digital media, graphic design tools, and marketing solutions. The evolution of Creative Cloud is a shining example of how the **Iterative** and **Innovative** mindset responded to industry shifts for Adobe.

Curiosity, Resilience, and Adaptability

Curiosity should be a component of **Iteration**, sparking questions like "What if?" and "How could this be done differently?" Building this into a team's DNA encourages experimentation, even when success is uncertain. It also means viewing setbacks as learning opportunities rather than reasons to hold back.

In an **Iterative** culture, resilience is developed by allowing teams to experiment safely with each **Iteration**. They know that each attempt contributes to the project's broader success regardless of its outcome.

Wait or Proceed?

One of the most challenging decisions for a leader in a rapidly evolving environment is whether to lead by **_Innovating_** or take a "wait-and-see" approach.

In some cases, a cautious approach can be beneficial. If an emerging technology seems promising but needs more established applications, it can be wise to wait and see. This approach allows others to spend their investment capital on the "trial and error" phase.

> ➜ *Think back to the beginning of the Internet search engine. Do you remember Wandex, Archie, WebCrawler, or Backrub? These were some of the first search engines designed by universities for academic purposes. Backrub evolved into Google about the time AltaVista was introduced. Shortly after, Microsoft threw its hat in the ring with MS Search.*
>
> *Eighty-five search engines were launched from 1993 to 2021. Today, when you need to search, you probably think of Google or Bing (Microsoft), yet forty-seven of the eighty-five search engines are still active. Many of the active ones are proprietary within larger websites like Yahoo.com.*

*In 1998, Larry Page and Sergey Brin, PhD candidates at Stanford University, decided to enter the market with a superior search engine called Google. After watching their predecessors' successes and failures, they **Envisioned** a fast, easy-to-use search engine for everyone.*

*They understood that you can only search digital content, so they began digitizing everything they could for their database. Their quest involved hundreds of **Iterations** of digitizing newspaper archives, novels, medical books, and more.* ←

Google keeps its search algorithms secret and constantly **Iterates** them. Today, Google performs more than 70% of internet searches.

Harnessing 5 Habits for Lasting Impact

Iteration without **Innovation** means repeating the same thing over and over. However, when **Innovation** is added, you learn from and build upon each **Iteration**. Then, your **Vision** blossoms beyond your expectations.

Mass Production may seem to break this rule. Mass production requires that the activity repeat the same results every time. But that doesn't mean that workers can't **Innovate** their attitude—simple things like bringing a picture of a personal **Vision** along with their lunch.

➜ *Ford Motor extended its assembly lines to build just about every component of the Model A car in the 1930s. However, workers struggled with the consistent repetition, and many left the company.*

The company was losing experienced workers, and production slowed while the replacements were in

*Henry Ford came up with an **Innovative** solution. He doubled the wages of all workers. They instantly became middle-class and could own a home and buy a car.*

The worker's attitude changed, and they loved their repetitive job! ⬅

Another Story of Innovative Success

➡️ *After World War II, Japanese companies became renowned for creating a culture of continuous improvement, or kaizen. This culture was deeply influenced by the introduction of employee-driven **Innovation** programs, where companies encouraged and rewarded employees for suggesting incremental improvements and new ways to enhance efficiency.*

Companies like Toyota, Sony, and Honda pioneered this approach by establishing formal suggestion systems and incentivizing workers to contribute ideas.

Toyota, for example, rewarded employees for suggestions that improved production processes. The success sprouted the lean manufacturing concept, which reduced waste and improved efficiency.

*These practices were crucial to Japan's post-war economic recovery and laid the foundation for the country's reputation for high-quality manufacturing and **Innovation**.*

*By valuing and rewarding incremental **Innovation**, Japanese companies fostered a culture where employees were consistently engaged in making improvements, no matter how small.*

This approach helped Japanese businesses achieve global competitiveness, showing that continuous, employee-driven improvement can lead to lasting success. ⬅️

Key Takeaways from this Chapter

- Create a positive learning environment.
- Use the 5 Habits Mindset for lasting results.
- Be intentional about **Innovation** and continual learning.
- Add curiosity and be adaptive.
- Be intentional about proceeding or waiting.
- Incentivize **Innovation** even in repetitive tasks or jobs.

Final Practice As You Learn

Google the "History of the Radio" and spend a few minutes following the evolution of radio technology and which company led each new wave.

Quick Quiz

On a scale of 1-5 (1=low, 5=high) rate yourself on these questions.

1-I am a curious person, always looking for ways to learn and **Innovate**.

1------2------3------4------5

2- I like to manage and minimize risks.

1------2------3------4------5

3- I practice continuous improvement.

1------2------3------4------5

4-I look for little ways to improve my life each day.

1------2 ----3------4------5

** If you feel a need to raise any of your scores, you know how to do it by now!

The 5 Habits for Change is the key to not just surviving but thriving in everything you do.

TURN
TO CLEAR
VISION

Chapter 11

11 - Okay, What's Next?

The 5 Habits for Change are Easy Mindsets to Remember

1-Iterate   Use the **Iterate** Habit to break your change project into manageable chunks. It's easier to work one step at a time. Using **Iterations**, the Change Journey will train you and your team to accomplish more, faster.

2-Vision   Expand your goals into emotion-filled **Visions** so that you, your team, friends, or family will understand the purpose and get enthused about the change.

3-Innovate   **Innovate** everywhere—the **Vision**, the **Project Plan**, improving the next **Iteration**, and the **Celebrations**.

4-Plan   Create a simple **Project Plan** on paper. Listing the project factors (**Vision**, required, activity, optional, celebrate) on paper makes it easy to organize an effective strategy.

5-Celebrate   **Celebrate** success at every step with an extra big **Celebration** at the end.

Here's How You'll Make Your Next Change Different Using the 5 Simple Habits for Successful Change

Habit 1 - ITERATE

You'll **ITERATE** by breaking your project into small incremental activities that progressively make the process work smarter.

Because it's easier to tackle small activities one at a time.

Habit 2 - VISION

You'll expand your Goals into dynamic **VISIONS**.

Because a Vision explains the why, the benefits, and is fun.

Habit 3 - INNOVATE

You'll **INNOVATE**, increasing the power of the 5 Habits.

Making the Change Journey Fun, Fast, and Effective for Everyone.

Habit 4 - PLAN

You'll create simple **PROJECT PLANS**.

Because it is your roadmap to successful change.

Habit 5 - CELEBRATE

You'll **CELEBRATE** each small accomplishment.

Because the project will be more fun and rewarding.

The End

Appendix

Our Thanks to Our Readers

Thanks for reading this book. We hope you had as much fun reading it as we did creating, **Iterating**, **Visioning**, **Innovating**, **Planning**, and **Celebrating**. We lost track of the number of **Iterations** we've worked through. Our original **Project Plan** went "fluid" early on as we discovered new ideas and reshaped the book for many **Iterations**.

We would also appreciate feedback, both good and bad. We'd love to hear your success story if it helped you with a problematic Change Project. Our website, www.5habitsForChange.com and Amazon has space for reviews.

May all your Change Journeys be Fun, Fast, and Effective.

Todd and *Gary*

www.5HabitsForChange.com

Turn Change into Your Competitive Advantage

Whether you're an individual navigating change, a leader guiding a team, or an organization driving transformation, the 5 Simple Habits for Successful Change will help you make every change fun, fast, and effective.

Change doesn't have to feel overwhelming. With our proven framework, you'll learn how to build momentum, engage others, and create lasting results— one simple habit at a time.

Four Ways We Can Help You Apply the 5 Habits:

- Engaging **Keynotes** that transform fear of change into excitement for what's next.

- **Workshops** (virtual or in-person) that energize your team and equip them with a proven formula for leading successful change.

- **Consulting** to guide your team or organization through real-world change.

- **Group & 1:1 Coaching** to help individuals and small teams make every change feel possible, purposeful, and doable.

To learn more about our products and services for individuals and organizations based on The 5 Simple Habits for Change visit:

www.5HabitsForChange.com

Author – Todd Musig

Todd Musig
BSBA, MBA

Todd Musig has spent over three decades empowering individuals and organizations to achieve greater focus, productivity, and balance. His career includes pivotal roles at renowned organizations such as FranklinCovey, Robbins Research International, AchieveGlobal, and Who Moved My Cheese? LLC. Alongside these accomplishments, Todd has successfully built and led several businesses, giving him firsthand experience navigating the complexities of leadership, teamwork, and strategy.

Todd is a sought-after speaker, consultant, and coach who has inspired audiences around the world. Known for his practical yet engaging approach, he shares proven strategies for mastering time, sharpening focus, boosting productivity, leading successful teams, and navigating change with confidence. Beyond the stage, Todd works closely with individuals and teams as a trusted coach, helping them cut through distractions and achieve what matters most in their work and lives.

Todd coauthors two additional books: *Juggling Elephants: An Easier Way to Get Your Most Important Things Done—Now!* and *Getting to It: Accomplishing the Important, Handling the Urgent, and Removing the Unnecessary*.

A devoted husband and father, Todd lives in Salt Lake City, Utah, with his wife and family. To learn more about Todd's books and services, visit www.toddmusig.com or connect with him on LinkedIn.

Author - Gary Dansie

Gary Dansie
MEd, MBA, MS

AAfter completing a BS in Marketing and an MEd from the University of Utah, Gary began his career in marketing. His clients included Fortune 500 companies and start-ups, but his real love was entrepreneurship.

Gary co-founded DIGOP, a Microsoft Gold Partner that specialized in building web software for the healthcare industry. DIGOP was later acquired by a publicly traded company. Another startup, Recovery Help, was the first fully telehealth addiction treatment accredited by the Joint Commission. He co-founded several other startups, some of which have been acquired and others that remain active today.

Because of his love for learning, he also completed an MBA and an MS in learning technology.

Through his clients, he has obtained insider access to the workings and cultures of dozens of organizations, ranging from International to startups to turnarounds.

While he lives in Salt Lake City with his wife, the world is his playground.

Our Appreciation

Thanks to all who helped us achieve our **Vision** of publishing this book.

Thanks to our many clients, who have allowed us to observe their organizations' processes and cultures, providing us with illustrative stories to share.

A big shout-out to Joe Price, LouAnn Bates, Rachel Pugmire, Alene McCrimmon, Mason Dansie, Todd Beck, Tim Brown, Jones Loflin, Zach Kristensen, Mike Smith, and others who previewed the book and pointed out "the good, the bad, and the ugly."

Their feedback helped us **Iterate** what you have just read.

Photo Credits

Illustrations

All illustrations by Gary Dansie

Introduction

Lightbulb   Photo by pphive2015 from Adobe Stock

Chapter 1 – Iterate the Change Journey

Arches   Photo by Robin Schreiner from Unsplash

Slinky Photo by Andy Roberts from iStock Photo

Football   Istock petesaloutos

Chapter 2 – Vision Spectacular Results

Seedling   Photo by BlackSalmon from iStock Photo

Jefferson   Image from Pixabay

Birds   Image by David Reed from Pixabay

Chapter 3 – Innovation Driven Change

Light Bulb   Image by S K from Pixabay

Cell Phones Mobil Phone Evolution 1992-2014.

Wikimedia Commons/public domain

Chapter 4 – Building a Simple Project Plan

Hopscotch   Photo by Jon Tyson fromUnsplash

Map   Image from Google Maps

Chapter 5-Celebrate

Firework   Photo by Gary Dansie

Chapter 6- Fine Tuning Results

Violin   Photo by Totoo G from Pixabay

Baguette   Photo by Luis Covarrubias on Unsplash

Wheat   Photo by Petra from Pixabay

Pizza Cook   Photo by Ugur Karakoc from iStock Photo

Chapter 7 – Pulling a Team Together

Rowers   Image by Sarah N from Pixabay

Pyramids   Image by Pete Linforth from Pixabay

Girl   Photo from Adobe Stock

Crowd   Photo from Adobe Stock

Chapter 8– Coach the Winning Team

Baseball   Image by Keith Johnston from Pixabay

Chapter 9 – Life Outside Work

Monkey   Image by Andre Mouton from Pixabay

Chapter 10 – A New Mindset for a Rapidly Changing World

Earth   Photo by Magann from Adobe Stock

Desert   Photo by Gary Dansie

Assembly Line The Ford assembly line in 1913. Wikimedia Commons/public domain

Chapter 11 – OK, What's Next?

Sunset   Image by Matt Noble from Pixabay